Praise for
"A Candle in the Heart"...

Judith Mannheimer Alter Kallman has written a compelling memoir, her story of a young child from Slovakia, who survived with only some of her siblings and has but dim memories of her parents and the beauty of a privileged, pious childhood. We journey with Judith from her native town through temporary havens and momentary respites into Hungary before the German invasion of March 1944 and then spend the final year of the Holocaust in German-occupied Budapest in a race between survival and death. Along the way we meet Jews who saved Jews, people who embraced a young, cute child as their own and others who turned their backs, so frozen by the dangers of their own situation that they could not care about an orphaned girl. The richness of the story is enhanced by the extensive description of the aftermath of the Holocaust, the kindness of Jews in England and then in the early years of the State of Israel, where Jewish children were raised and rehabilitated in villages which healed the body and nourished the soul. *A Candle in the Heart*, Judith's story, is well worth telling and is told so well.

Michael Berenbaum, Ph.D.
Director of the Sigi Ziering Center for the
Study of the Holocaust and Ethics

It was once fittingly said of Eleanor Roosevelt that she 'would rather light a candle than curse the darkness.' The same could be said of Judith Kallman. In her deeply moving and profoundly courageous memoir, *A Candle in the Heart*, she illuminates the goodness of the human spirit amidst the darkness of the Holocaust. She illustrates in haunting detail the human capacity for unspeakable cruelty and evil, but more importantly, she reminds us that light—which is seen through her love for family and friends, the selfless sacrifice of strangers, and the sustaining power of faith—can endure and prevail even in the darkest moments of human history. *A Candle in the Heart* reminds us all that hope is eternal.

Senator Joseph Lieberman (I-CT)

Kallman's story as a child survivor of the Holocaust is heart wrenching and inspirational...a poignant memoir of the triumph of the human spirit, renewal, and faith. This book is for all who believe in the power of family, the importance of inspiring future generations to keep the light of Judaism bright, and to cherish the memory of those who perished in the Holocaust.

Jacob Dayan
Consul General of Israel

This is an emotionally powerful and riveting story of an awesome display of heroism in the face of some of the most egregious and cruel acts against humanity.

Peter Tesei
First Selectman (R-Greenwich, CT)

"It was impossible to put this book down. I thought I was reading fiction as the drama was riveting, inspirational and very moving—A TRIUMPH, A MUST READ."

Leon H. Charney
The Charney Report, *NYC-TV*

A Candle in the Heart

Memoir of a Child Survivor

Judith Alter Kallman

Wordsmithy, LLC

2011

Published by
Wordsmithy, LLC
New Milford, NJ 07646
www.thewordsmithy.com

cover design by
Jeff Coen | JDC Design

ISBN: 978-1-935110-10-1 (hc)
978-1-935110-09-5 (pb)

Library of Congress Registration Number
TX 7-424-302

A Candle in the Heart

IS DEDICATED
TO MY PAST, PRESENT, AND FUTURE.

In memory of Jonah and Dora Mannheimer, my parents,
and Robi and Rena Mannheimer, my sister and brother
who were murdered during the Holocaust.

To Howard Alter, my first husband,
and to my brother, Asher.
Their lives were cut short too soon
for them to discover all of life's beauty.

⚜

To Irwin, the anchor of my life; and my true love.

⚜

To my children, who are my strength and courage;
Deborah and Mark, Jonathan, Robert and Shari,
Patti and Rob, Jonathan and Bryanna.

To my grandchildren and great-grandchildren;
Stephanie, Melissa, Evan, Eric, Chelsea, Alyson,
Kyle, Kevin, Austin, Alexa, Samantha, Bryan,
Jason, Ethan, Sam and Jack.

They enrich my life daily, hold our beautiful
traditions in their hands
and are true to it always.

TABLE OF CONTENTS

— Judith Mannheimer Alter Kallman

ACKNOWLEDGMENTS

This book is the fulfillment of my obligation as a child survivor of the Holocaust. It has long been my dream to make this book a reality, and its creation relied on the steadfast encouragement and help offered by my family and friends. Without them, it would not exist. Without them, I could never have put my experiences and the lessons I learned into words for others to absorb. It is a book about what can happen when we assume that nothing can happen, and it is a celebration of life, of our triumph over the forces of evil.

As an adult, I discovered that life is indeed beautiful and that I can enjoy my family and love deeply. I owe that ability to my parents, Jonah and Dora, of blessed memory, who lavished the best of their love, hope and care upon me from the moment I appeared in their lives. After they were taken, the nurturing from their hearts was my comfort through all the horror that followed. How does one say "thank you" for that? I do it by remembering what they did for me and by writing it all down for my own children and their descendants.

Long ago, because of what I went through, I decided that children must know that not every child lives a safe and secure life, and they must be taught to empathize with those children who do have losses and try to understand their pain. Children need a reminder that children are not always protected, that everywhere in this world, at this very moment, there are vulnerable children and that it is our duty to reach out and protect them.

The least I can do to raise awareness, I thought, was to put my story on the record and make my history come alive. Perhaps, somewhere, someone will take the lessons of my life to heart and make a difference.

My family has been deeply involved in this process, and I want to acknowledge that most of all. It took more than ten years to create what you hold in your hands, and they read each draft, over and over again, until we were all satisfied with the final version. I am grateful for their love, patience, advice and honesty.

My daughter, Debbie, was instrumental from the start. Without her determination, constant help and strength, this book would never have been written.

My children claim that the survivor in me has always been trying to reach the child I once was. By writing this book, I think the two have come together at last.

While the first seeds of inspiration came from the need to remember and set down my story, the second inspiration came from Professor Elie Wiesel, the Holocaust survivor who won the Nobel Peace Prize. "How do I tell my story?" I asked Wiesel when we met.

"Just sit down and start writing," he answered.

And I did.

I want to acknowledge Holocaust scholars Dr. Michael Berenbaum, Ari Goldman, Laura Slutsky, Susanna Margolis and Dr. Mordecai Paldiel. Special thanks to Carolyn Starman Hessel of the National Jewish Book Council for believing in my book.

My appreciation also goes to my brother, Bubi/Moshe Mannheimer, and my sister, Bella Katz, who helped fill gaps in my memory.

Most of all, I would like to thank my editor Jeanette Friedman, who worked endlessly with me to make this book a reality.

Books have permanence, and this book gives voice to my beloved parents, to my lost brother and sister, and to the millions of souls cruelly destroyed by hatred. May their memories be a blessing to us all.

My beloved Irwin says this work is a testimonial to courage and faith, rebirth and new life. I thank him with all my heart for supporting this effort with his patience, understanding, and his endless love.

Judith Mannheimer Alter Kallman
Greenwich, Connecticut, May 2011

FOREWORD

As a college student, I took a political science course to study the approaches and tactics used by individuals to transform the political world. A course requirement was to write about a leader and assess his impact on a particular aspect of society. I wanted to examine how, during World War II and the Holocaust, Adolf Hitler affected the lives of Jewish children — perhaps because there was a perfect case study in my own home — that of my mother, Judith Mannheimer Alter Kallman, whose story is told in this book.

My mother's life was deeply affected by the actions Hitler set in motion to solve "the Jewish problem." As the youngest of her nuclear family, and as part of an extended family that spread across Slovakia and Hungary, she is a perfect example of a child survivor of the Holocaust.

My research consisted of interviewing my mother and investigating the places and events that were germane to her story. The process proved to be a soul-wrenching experience for her, as it opened up memories that had been tucked away in the crevices of her heart. She was forthcoming nevertheless, and despite the pain, let her mind travel back to the pleasant moments of childhood and then on to the torturous years of hiding, fear, and loss.

The time I spent with my mother—when the repressed thoughts of a lifetime were finally unleashed—were defining moments that created an exceptional intimacy between us. It reaffirmed our belief in the importance of family and in the bedrock of our Judaism.

For both of us, my college research paper became a true labor of love, and I thank my mother for opening her heart and allowing me the opportunity to learn in such detail about her childhood. Significantly, my Professor John Chambers' comments included a note of thanks to my mother for allowing him to read such a direct and moving story, one that affected him greatly. For this book, which began with that research paper so many years ago, I thank my mother even more. I believe, like my college professor does, that her readers will be grateful to her for telling us her story.

I know it has not been easy, and it has taken many years to complete, but I also know how determined she has been to bring this book into being. And when it is a question of having determination, my mother has few peers. Determination helped my mother survive—it was not just her desire or will to live that kept her going, it was also her insistence that she had no option but to choose life.

That determination has always been my mother's greatest strength, and I believe it is why, from her youth to today, she has always defied the odds in overcoming her adversaries and life's challenges. When so few children survived the Holocaust, Mom survived and built on each of her experiences to strengthen her resolve to go forward. Now, she is resolutely determined to put her book into the hands of children everywhere.

All my mother really had in those days was her faith, her recollection of the warmth of her family, and a sense of self. She relied on those beliefs, memories and emotions; in a very real sense, they grew stronger with time. And as you will read, that strength kept her alive and forged the optimism with which she still regards the world.

My mother has transferred this positive energy to her children and grandchildren. It explains why she is our family's pillar of strength, our link to our past, our hopeful believer in the future, and our tower of love.

Though decades have passed since we sat down and did the interviews for my research paper, my mother has written and edited this book in her mind many times over. She has finally put her story down on paper, and her dream has become a reality.

Deborah Alter Goldenberg
Los Angeles, April 2011

INTRODUCTION

My memories are lit from within by the golden glow of the Sabbath candles, the most potent image of my early childhood. When the haven that had been my family was destroyed, when my parents' loving protection was ripped from me and my childhood innocence had been nullified, I carried that light in my heart. Then, as now, the flame kindled hope inside me, and kept my soul warm.

In the summer of 1995, my granddaughter Alyson, then five years old, came to stay with me for two weeks. At the time, her family—my daughter Debbie, her husband Mark Goldenberg, and Alyson's three siblings—were traveling in Eastern Europe. Their tour was intended specifically to explore the cities and towns that had once been home to the thriving pre-World War II Jewish civilization in Europe and to visit the ghettos, camps, and crematoria in which that civilization had been destroyed.

Clearly, such a trip was not appropriate for a five-year-old. Alyson would not have understood what she was seeing. Unable to appreciate the tracing of history —

Alyson Goldenberg.

and too young to be subjected to knowledge of its cruelty — she would have been bored and fidgety. So it was settled. She would stay with me and my husband Irwin since we could be counted on to lavish loving attention upon her. Debbie arranged for swimming lessons and play dates for her little girl, promised to phone frequently, and left.

When you are five, two weeks is a lifetime. When the youngest of four siblings in a vibrant and busy household comes to the home of much older people — even if they are her grandparents — it can be a wrenching experience. And so for the first two days, Alyson was like a stone. She never complained. She agreed to every suggestion. She accepted every demonstration of affection. But sadness covered her like a shroud. The only joy came from the the time she'd spend at the local Chabad daycare center, where she loved being with other children.

At meal times, I tried my best to speak gaily of all our plans for her, but her dark eyes were doleful, and their melancholy broke my heart. At night, she would lie very still in her bed, and while she seemed to listen when I lay beside her and read to her, sleep wouldn't come unless Irwin sat with her and stroked her hand gently and endlessly until fatigue overcame her. She was unreachable, and I could not understand why I didn't have the power to lessen her pain. Nor could I fathom why her pain and my impotence were causing me such distress. On the third day, my daughter phoned from Poland. She spoke first to Alyson, then to me. That day, a Friday, she and her family had gone to Auschwitz, where my parents and my two older siblings had been taken so long ago—the place where they were murdered in 1942.

As I spoke to Debbie, Alyson sat at the kitchen table, her head on her arms, looking at me with soulful, sad eyes.

Debbie told me she stood in front of the gas chambers in that place and recited the Kaddish (the prayer for the dead) for my family—who were torn away from me when I was Alyson's age. "Mom," Debbie said to me, "I felt their presence. I felt their souls come down to me."

When Debbie told me what she had done, the trauma flooded over me once more. I lost my sense of self and found myself weeping uncontrollably for those I had lost.

In a flash I understood Alyson's pain. In that instant, when the spirit of my dead family seemed to be burning down the telephone wires across oceans and continents and decades, I recognized my granddaughter's anguish. I had experienced the same sense of utter bereavement.

Alyson's "abandonment" was benign and would end in two weeks, mine was a separation ruthlessly enforced and stretched through a lifetime. But regardless of circumstances, the child's feeling was the same: the five-year-old's uncomprehending sense of being orphaned, adrift, and homeless. Alyson's pain was the same as the pain I try so hard to suppress. It surfaced in me, as I looked at her, with Debbie's voice in my ear.

Debbie's phone call from Auschwitz came on Sabbath eve. The Sabbath's unchanging rituals have always been a constant in our family. On Friday nights, the closeness and warmth of Jewish tradition created a snug, safe harbor for the little girl I was, for the woman I became, and for the family I created.

As I wished Debbie a *Shabbat Shalom*, a wish for peace, I noticed Alyson's ears perk up. It was a familiar greeting that in some small way gave her comfort.

Debbie couldn't see Alyson but sensed an opening. "Mom," she said, "Be sure to light candles with Alyson tonight."

In this hour of her unhappiness, her mom realized that *Shabbat* candles were a touchstone for Alyson and a connection with the family she missed so much. "We'll light candles tonight," I promised Alyson when I got off the phone. "Would that make you happy?"

"Yes, Grandma," she said. "But can we go shopping first?"

I laughed and hugged Alyson with all my might. She cheered up immediately when I assured her that we'd do both: shop and light candles. I laughed because my experience of abandonment and hers were — thankfully — so different. And I realized that even if I didn't have the security I needed as a child, at least I had survived and could provide it to the ones I love. That, too, is a gift; that, too, is a victory.

CHAPTER ONE
The Tapestry of Generations

When most people remember their parents, they summon a tapestry of recollections — the fabric of their memory is woven from the intertwined threads of sights, sounds, smells, textures, tastes, and events embroidered into the design of their lives.

Many of these sons and daughters are gifted with a sense of their parents as individuals. They know what made their parents laugh and what made them angry. They remember their mother's and father's distinctive temperaments and elicit at will the elusive, ineffable characters and personalities of each. So richly varied and deeply planted are the memories of their parents, that years later and miles away it takes only a hint of a fragrance, a taste of food, a snippet of song or a certain smile to instantly transport them to their parented, safe, loving childhoods.

I own no such tapestry. When I lost my parents to the Germans and their Slovakian collaborators, I was too young to experience much of their personalities or character beyond knowing that my most basic needs were being met — a child's perception of what it meant to be loved and secure. I remember my parents' smiles, but even those were infrequent. That was because by the time I came along — the last of six children — there was less and less to smile about.

I will never know my mother's favorite color, my father's favorite dish, or what kind of music my parents liked. I will never know how they relaxed in the evenings or whether they went to the theater. Did they enjoy reading? What were their political beliefs? Did they adore the ballet as I do? Did they enjoy sports as I do? Did they love art and have a talent for it, as I seem to?

I never had a chance to hear my parents tell the stories of their own childhoods. They never got to tell me about their sisters and brothers; what it was like to grow up; what their parents were like, and how they lived their day-to-day lives. Did they love the warm weather or relish cold winters? Did they have a favorite holiday? What did they drink? Did they ever quarrel? What did their laughter sound like? I'll never know these things. I'll never know the answers to a million questions, small and large, that have occurred to me day after day, year after year.

Some facts of their brief lives form the basis of the family tapestry that I began to weave anew — they define its size and mark its edges, but they are not fully woven into it. My surviving siblings and cousins have passed along reminiscences that are tantalizing points of color, but there are only a few. Who can know how the many-colored threads my parents held within might have enhanced our lives? Their loss is deep, irretrievable, and incomprehensible.

We lived in Piešt'any, Czechoslovakia in what was soon to become Slovakia. (In territorial turmoil since the end of World War I, the Czech and Slovakian elements that had formed Czechoslovakia were in the process of being torn apart by the rise of German power.)

In the summer of 1938, Piešt'any had some 15,000 residents, of whom approximately 1,500 were Jewish. The town was a well-known resort harkening back to Roman times and was situated in a region that was primarily farmland organized into feudal estates worked by a local peasantry.

Piešt'any is a lovely place, a riverbank town with ample parkland and its own swimming pool. It was fairly busy; a large train station accommodated spa-

Piešt'any Town Square.

The Spa in Piešťany.

The Crystal Bridge.

goers from all over Europe who came to seek relief from the aches of arthritis and rheumatism. They often passed the time between treatments strolling through the lively town square. Majestic mountains surrounded the valley, and there were public gardens filled with flowers everywhere.

Pieštany's main spa was located on an island in the river that ran through the town and was connected to the town center by a beautiful, roofed and etched crystal bridge, famous throughout Europe. During the Second World War the glass panes were removed and never replaced, but they were not destroyed, and they are now on display in the Pieštany Museum. I remember walking across that bridge with my family, especially in the summertime.

I don't know if my great-great-grandfather, David Lev Mannheimer, lived among the first fifty Jewish families in Pieštany, but I do know he was born in sub-Carpathia in 1785. He is the first Mannheimer we know of in the family, the first in the direct line that descends through me to my children, my grandchildren and the generations to come.

My great-great uncle, Gaon Rav Chaim Tzvi Mannheimer (1814-1886), was the leader of the Jewish community, exceptionally learned in Judaism and brilliant in his judgments — hence the title *gaon*, high praise for a Talmudic genius. In addition to being a Jewish leader, his advice and counsel were often sought by the civic leaders in Ungvar, a major city 300 miles away. His nephew Moshe Mordechai (1856-1926) was my grandfather, who married Fani Leah Fisher (1862-1938).

Moshe Mordechai ran a successful general store and sold all sorts of goods to the workers from the surrounding farms and to the tourists flocking to Piešťany's spas. As an observant Jew, he maintained the scholarly tradition of his famous uncle by studying Torah in his spare time. You would always find my grandfather with his nose buried in an open book during his spare moments. This sense of dual responsibility — to business and to Torah scholarship — is something Moshe Mordechai would pass onto his son, my father Jonah, in ample measure.

After the First World War, the future must have looked promising to the Jews living in Piešťany. Their homeland was a nation whose capital, Prague, had a century before been home to one of the largest Jewish populations in all of Europe, a capital that had given the world the likes of Franz Kafka, Max Brod, and Franz Werfel, all brilliant stars in the firmament of 20th century literature, all of them Jews.

Even a small Jewish community like ours felt the stirrings of new ideas. Zionism inspired numbers of young people, some of whom immigrated to British Mandate Palestine. Others joined the newly organized Agudath Israel, a non-Zionist Orthodox religious movement, and some rejected religion entirely, becoming socialists and communists. The creativity that animated Jewish life was also unleashed on the business front — and business was good. In what was Czechoslovakia before World War II Jews were pioneers of the nation's economic development and an important engine of its success. Jewish firms took the lead in mining northern Bohemia, in the steel industry, in insurance and banking. Individual Jews were particularly prominent in the textile, foodstuffs, wood, and paper industries.

When riots flared against Piešťany's small but prosperous Jewish community in October 1920, the president of the National Federation of Czechoslovak Jews appealed to President Tomáš Garrigue Masaryk himself to deal with the situation. Legend has it that my grandfather, a highly respected leader of the Jewish community, was formally elected as its representative, and sent to greet Masaryk when he came to Piešťany for talks.

Our Jewish community was buoyed by a supportive liberal voice at the very head of the government and sustained by a long benign history in the region, one that allowed Jews to worship undisturbed and to make a living without restraint or restriction. By the time my father courted and married my mother and brought her to Piešťany in 1928, the young couple would have assumed that they could raise their family in safety and comfort for eternity.

Eugen (Jonah) Mannheimer was born in 1894 in Piešťany. He was the second youngest of thirteen children born to Moshe Mordechai and Fani, though one of his siblings did not survive childhood. He was tall, square-jawed, and very handsome, with

Eugen Jonah Mannheimer.

reddish-blond hair that has been passed on to one of my grandsons. He was also a successful businessman, fluent in several languages, and learned in the Torah. He was a stylish man who traveled the region, buying and selling goods for his father's general store. Everyone liked his pleasant personality and enjoyed his company. Like his father before him, when he could find the time, you would find him reading a newspaper, book or studying Torah.

As was the custom in those days, when my father reached the age to marry, he had to meet the right girl. The way to wrangle an introduction to an "appropriate" young lady was through a matchmaker, especially in the somewhat closed and strictly patriarchal Orthodox Jewish community. Such introductions, steeped in tradition, were standard, and for many young adults was the only way to meet a member of the opposite sex.

My grandmother Fani was a very clever woman who, knowing she would have to find appropriate spouses for her children, didn't want to limit her children's choices to the offerings of local matchmakers—who also demanded steep fees. So she opened a successful café next door to the spa, and thereby met many wealthy people from all over Europe whose sons and daughters might be suitable matches and those who could recommend potential mates. Eventually, all her children made good marriages.

By the time my father met my mother, he was already in his early 30s, and logic dictates that he had worked his way through the appropriate young ladies in Pieštany and its environs without finding Miss Right. Perhaps one of Fani's customers suggested that Jonah travel to the Hungarian city of Vác to meet a lovely young lady by the name of Dora Ungar. We will never know how they came to meet or who introduced them. What we do know is that Jonah went to Hungary in 1927 or 1928 — a journey of 80 miles as the crow flies — to meet the beautiful Dora.

My mother was the youngest of five. Born in Vác in 1904, she, like my father, stemmed from a prestigious line of rabbis and scholars. Her father, Jonash Ungar, was the grandson of a rabbi, and her mother, Ethel Neumann, was the granddaughter of Gaon Rab Anshel Neumann.

Vác sits on the Danube, a little over 12 miles north of Budapest. My maternal grandparents owned a thriving shoe business there and lived in a comfortable house with a very large garden and orchard out back. The land was filled with a variety of berry bushes and fruit trees, and my grandmother lovingly tended to her vegetables and flowers by herself. Their home was the weekend gathering place of all the family — my mother's older siblings, their spouses and children made a lively, happy brood. It was so comfortable and secure, that my mother, with her newborn cradled in her arms, would return to Vác after each delivery. Of course, I was too young to remember that trip, but in later years and darker times I would find some comfort in picking and feasting on fresh, ripe, sweet-scented and juicy berries — raspberries, blackberries, gooseberries and strawberries. They tasted of sunshine and dew.

Dora Ungar Mannheimer.

By all accounts, my mother was a beauty and she'd won a local beauty contest. Everyone who ever spoke to me about her—close family members, friends and some who knew her only in passing—always said that she was a fine-looking woman. At 24, when my father met her, she was exquisite. She was also well-educated, was fluent in German and Hungarian, and loved poetry. A cousin remembers lying beside her in a meadow one hot, bright summer day, listening as Mama recited her favorite poems.

Papa was ten years older than she was, but that was no barrier, for the beauty he met in Vác captured his heart, and he captured hers. They were married in her hometown on December 12, 1928. Then he triumphantly brought her to Piešťany, where his family was smitten by her abilities and her charms, welcoming her into their hearts.

My parents lived with my paternal grandparents in the family's two-story house on Štefánikova Ulice (Street), a house taller than the buildings on either side of it. My grandparents, Mordechai Moshe and Fani, lived downstairs and we lived on the second floor. There was a park at one end of our street, and a hotel right across from us. It served tourists, conference attendees, and traveling salesmen. Not far from our house was the synagogue our family attended.

From the street all you could see of our house was a beige-colored stucco wall with huge, off-center, heavy, double wooden doors and some windows. There was no way to know what was behind those doors, but once you gained entry, you found yourself in a large

My parents on their wedding day, December 12, 1928.

My parents go for a stroll.

courtyard. There was a woodshed toward the back, and gardens for vegetables and flowers. The well was in the courtyard, too.

The building had black wrought iron railings that ran along the continuous stone balconies on each of the two stories. A short flight of masonry steps led to side-by-side big, heavy wooden doors for the two apartments.

I remember the first floor apartment, because by the time I was born in the late summer of 1937, we were living in it. The main door opened into a parlor. Beyond it was the dining room, with windows facing the street. There were three bedrooms — one for the boys, one for the girls, and one for my parents. There was also a tiny room for the maid. The furniture was a fine Victorian style, and I do remember that the highly polished and carved dining room table was about nine feet long!

Our house on Stefanikova Ulice (Street).

Mama takes us for a walk.

Although there was a well in the yard, we also had indoor plumbing—a toilet and a sink. I also remember a bathtub and water being heated for it on the kitchen stove, but I can't remember if the bathtub was fixed to the floor in the kitchen or brought in when needed.

The community into which my mother came as a bride was a community anchored in faith and in the rituals of Jewish life. Not that she had all that much time to get settled: my mother began having babies right away. A cousin remembers her as being "always pregnant."

My sister, Isabella (Bella), was born a year after the wedding; Morris (Moshe), nicknamed Bubi, arrived next. Arthur (Asher), whom we called Turi, was born after that. Then came my sister Rena (Rachel). Robi (Shmuel) followed her, and I, Judita, whom they called Blimeleh—Yiddish for "little flower"—was the last to arrive.

For some of these births, my mother traveled to a lying-in hospital in Bratislava, but I was born in Pieštany, in the large hospital that still sits beside the river.

While the older children attended school, we little ones, who were never left alone, played in the courtyard or in the park at the end of our street. Hide-and-seek was our favorite game. Mama, always busy, hired a woman who served as our nanny and housekeeper.

Most of my father's family lived near Pieštany and came for visits, especially during the summer, when it seemed like our extended family was vast and global.

(l-r) Judith, Robi, Rena, Turi, Bubi and Bella.

Unfortunately, these visits happened too early in my life to be imprinted on my memory, and the sense I have is that those were very happy times. We spoke Czech in school and at home, and my parents spoke Hungarian and German to each other.

I was a skinny little girl with huge green eyes, who resembled my father. In a house that was always fragrant with the smells of Mama's cooking—she loved to serve us hearty soups, delicious cakes, yeasty breads, and crispy pastries—I was a reluctant eater and difficult to tempt. Since food was so important, and babies needed to be chubby to be considered healthy, I remember my parents hovering over me, urging me to eat "a little more, a little more." My refusal to eat certainly earned me their time and attention.

Mama also paid close attention to the details of every aspect of our lives. In addition to being well-fed, the children of a family of our social stature were always supposed to be well-behaved, neat and clean. Mama took great pride in dressing us in fashionable clothing she designed herself, and had local tailors and dressmakers make them for us from the finest fabrics.

We would line up like chicks on either side of Mama in our matching outfits. Mama, though her waistline was understandably thickened by six pregnancies in eight years, would wear classically tailored tweed walking-suits that would be stylish even today. Everyone would comment on what a beautiful family we were. In time, my parents would strive to downplay their material success, but in those first years of my life we simply enjoyed it.

Despite the degree of tolerance and under-standing that prevailed, Jews and Gentiles in Piešťany lived separate lives. Social interaction between the two groups was minimal and, on the surface, harmonious. Jews had learned from long experience that to keep the deeply rooted antisemitism that lay just below the surface at bay, separation and civility were best. My parents and their neighbors thus treated one another with neighborly friendliness and respect, yet they kept their distance. We employed non-Jews at home and in the business, and Papa dealt routinely with a clientele that consisted of townspeople, peasants from the countryside, and tourists, but he never became too familiar with them.

Reluctant to attend secular schools, the religiously observant Jewish community of Piešťany had its own elementary school run by Dr. Alexander Mittelmann, attended by my siblings, and that's why their friends were almost exclusively Jewish.

Bella, my older sister, told me that she would often walk across the bridge to the spa island with her girlfriends to visit a small zoo that displayed an exotic collection of birds. She also remembers that when the weather was good, Mama would take us to a gazebo where we would sit with townspeople and tourists to listen to orchestras playing waltzes, marches, and the classics. Life was good.

Grandfather Moshe Mordechai died in 1929, just after Bella was born. She remembers that when Grandmother Fani died she was laid out on the floor of the house, with her head resting on a brick, surrounded by lit candles. She was buried after the Sabbath, on a Sunday, in the grand style of the family matriarch. Family members traveled overnight from all over Europe to pay their last respects.

After her funeral, we moved from our smaller apartment on the second floor to her very spacious apartment downstairs. We often rented the spare rooms upstairs to tourists taking the waters, or used them as guest rooms for our numerous relatives. In a veritable tribe of lively folk, my parents were everyone's favorite aunt and uncle. Family members told me that they loved to spend time with my parents because they were kind people and fun to be with.

I spent most of my time in the kitchen, where Mama spent her days cooking and baking, moving from the sturdy wooden worktable to the stove and back again. I often played under that table, and remember being lifted and placed upon it so my ears could be inspected before Mama cleaned them. Mama would warm up some oil then place a few drops in my ear to melt the wax. Then she would clean my ears out. It tickled a lot. She was always patient with us, and never seemed to suffer from stress. She was a happy woman.

That table was also where my older brothers and sisters did their homework. When they struggled with geometry, Mama would take time from her cooking to help them with their lessons. I liked to imitate them and pretend that I, too, had homework. I would scribble my own version of triangles, parallelograms and formulae on a piece of scrap paper with a bit of pencil—a little girl fantasizing about growing up and studying in her own right.

In many ways, the first years of my life—those all-important formative years—were as normal, as comfortable, and as secure as any child could wish for. Only years later did I come to understand how increasingly difficult it must have been for my parents to maintain such normality. A storm of hate was brewing; the war had begun, though we children did not know it. It was coming over the hills and up the river and would soon be in our town, on our street, outside our door.

Yet within our walls, at least for me, all was well.

Jewish holidays, whether the New Year (Rosh Hashana), the festival of Tabernacles (Sukkoth), or Passover (*Pesach*) were always special—and what fun it was to anticipate them! We children knew everything would be exceptionally delicious and different. Weeks in advance, we were fitted for new clothes and new shoes, but could not wear those items until the holiday arrived. When relatives and friends from near and far would arrive in joyful crowds at our house, we knew the holiday was upon us.

Mama worked extra hard to make our house shine and prepared extra special foods. For Sukkoth, we would cover a portion of the courtyard with a tarpaulin and create the *sukkah*—a ramshackle booth made of old doors, covered with a roof of reeds or evergreens. These little sheds commemorated the temporary shelters of our ancestors during the Exodus, and were decorated with brightly colored paper chains and hanging fruit. For a full week, rain or shine, the *sukkah* was where we ate our meals. I always loved those days and remember picking pine needles out of my chicken soup whenever the wind blew.

The Sabbath (*Shabbat*) was an essential part of my formative years. For whatever might have been happening outside — and even in the early years terrible things were beginning to happen — celebrating it every Friday night and Saturday was an absolute given, an unwavering, unchanging, fixed ritual in our lives.

Papa was often away for most of the week, traveling on business, but he was always home in time for the Sabbath. When he was gone, I missed him terribly, and took comfort in knowing that when Friday night arrived it meant Papa would be home, taking his rightful place as patriarch of our clan at the head of our table.

The Sabbath was a gift out of time, a special, shining moment that illumined the safe, secure, loving boundaries of my world. And it brought with it traditions and rituals that are with me still.

Though we lived in a fairly modern town, there were no kitchen appliances, washing machines or dryers. Most homes didn't even have proper ovens for baking, which meant families relied on the local baker's oven to bake their bread dough, including special braided challah breads, and to cook the *cholent*, a steamy, aromatic, garlicky stew — the main dish for Saturday lunch.

We, on the other hand, had a good stove for baking, and on Friday mornings the aroma of fresh-baked challah floated from Mama's efficient kitchen, filling a house that had been scrubbed until it shone. When Mama was done cleaning the house, she made sure her children were clean, too, and then decked us out in our finery—the boys in starched shirts and collars, the girls in our prettiest dresses—cautioning us to be very careful not to make a mess.

Bubi would carry the family's *cholent* pot to the bakery on Friday afternoons, where it was placed in the oven next to myriad pots prepared by our neighbors. (Each pot had a family "trademark" so that you could easily identify your own pot on the way home from the synagogue on Saturday morning. It would be served, steaming hot, as the main course for lunch.)

As sunset approached, my sisters and I would help Mama spread her best white damask tablecloth, edged with hand-crocheted lace, on the large dining room table. We set it with Mama's gleaming silver candlesticks and Papa's huge *Kiddush* cup, a wine goblet so big, it rested on its own special stand. Mama used her finest china, crystal glassware, and silver flatware to honor the day of peace and rest.

After all the hectic preparations, as the sun dipped below the horizon, our shining, loving, close-knit family would stand quietly around the beautifully set table as Mama covered her thick ebony hair with a pure white lace mantilla and lit eight candles, one for each of us. When each flame burned bright and the glow filled the dining room, she would tent her hands over the candlesticks and sweep their light toward her face — three times in succession, with slow and graceful movements.

I would watch, wide-eyed, as she covered her eyes to recite the blessing in Hebrew. When she finished, she would open her eyes, turning to hug her daughters. I would press up against the wonderful warmth of her body and gaze into those, dark, loving eyes. Decades later, when I close my eyes, I can bask in that look — and wonder now if she hid her fear for us behind it.

Then the "men" (meaning my father and the boys) would leave for the synagogue. When they returned an hour or so later, they brought with them a hint of the cool outdoor air as they stepped into the peaceful apartment. We loved watching our handsome Papa, in his dark suit, his glittery gold watch chain looped across his dark vest, take his place in the throne-like armchair at the head of our table.

We children lined up like little soldiers, in chronological order, to receive his paternal blessing. I was always the last, filled with sweet, heady anticipation as I waited my turn. I impatiently wanted my special moment with Papa. At last, he would reach down, lift me onto his lap and hold me tight. I would cuddle closer to his broad chest, as he enfolded me in his embrace. "May the Lord bless you and protect you," he would recite gently in Hebrew. "May the Lord countenance you and be gracious unto you. May the Lord favor you and grant you peace."

Then we would silently return to our places and remain standing. Papa would rise from his "throne" and pour deep, rich, red wine into the shining silver

Kiddush cup. He would slowly lift it in one hand, holding his prayer book in the other, and chant the prayer to sanctify the wine. He knew the words by heart, the *Kiddush* prayer flowing smoothly from his lips. When he was done, he would sit down, and sip from the cup. Silently he would pass the cup to Mama, who took a sip, and then the cup was passed to each of us in turn. Before the meal continued, we would wash our hands for Mama's braided challah bread, which Papa blessed, and then cut and distributed to each of us. We would make the blessing before we popped the delicious, eggy, sweet bread into our mouths. Then Mama would bring forth her delicious fish dishes, soups, chickens and compotes. We ate as we shared stories about our week and sang Sabbath songs with great joy. Those peaceful and happy times are engraved in my memory.

After lunch on Saturdays, the Jewish families of Piešťany would take leisurely strolls through the town's picturesque streets or gather on the benches that lined the banks of the river. Papa often walked us across the crystal bridge to the spa island or took us to the local park near the town square, where water fountains spouted the foul-smelling mineral water that made Piešťany so famous. In his pockets he carried sugar cubes

A modern-day Judith at one of Piešťany's water fountains.

and would hand one to each of us as he pushed the button on the water fountain while urging us to drink. I can still smell and taste that unpleasant water to this day, but because Papa asked, I drank it, holding the sugar cube on my tongue so that the sweetness would counteract the awful taste of the water. I did not know then that sweetness and bitterness are the flavors that stay with us for our lifetimes.

Even as a great-grandmother today, every Sabbath I light my own candles and bask in their glow. I feel I am once again in Papa's arms. I feel utter tranquility within, a sense of perfect protection, of being completely enveloped in love. It is a feeling I will never lose; it is a memory so strong, brilliant, and vital that its power still moves me.

When I watch my son and son-in-law bless their children with the same blessing Papa gave us, with the exact words and gestures that have been handed down to our people for thousands of years, it is as if I am watching an old movie shot through gauze and misty around the edges. The image of my son dissolves into that of my father; my grandchildren become my siblings. Loss is trumped by fulfillment, by the sense of continuity, by the triumph of my children following the tradition of their ancestors.

That is when I appreciate the power of my father's blessing for me. It worked. Time after time, God reached down from His Heaven to keep me alive as I carried my family's Sabbath candle light in my heart wherever I went. It was my source of hope and warmth—even when all hope seemed chilled by a cold, cold world.

Chapter Two
A Rock Through the Window

Iremember the first time hooligans destroyed the peace of our Friday nights. To anyone looking in from outside, the dining room window facing the street framed an intimate, radiant tableau of our family — Papa holding the silver cup that reflected the light of the candles; Mama in her bright white mantilla, and six well-mannered children in a row, awaiting Papa's precious blessing.

Suddenly a rock was hurled through the window with frightening force, shattering it and our *Sabbath* peace. The window exploded with a cracking snap and splintered into thousands of flying shards, as the crude missile landed with a loud bang on the floor. Screams ripped from our throats; everyone instinctively ducked, and I threw myself under the table. None of us knew what was happening. We were confused and panicked. What could possibly have triggered such an event?

As a very young child I was unaware of the forces of history working to tear the world all around me to

The Hlinka Guard (courtesy USHMM).

bits. I was just a tyke when Hitler's troops marched unopposed into the Sudentenland on October 1, 1938. Soon what was Czechoslovakia began to break up. Southern Slovakia and Ruthenia were annexed by Hungary; the Zaolzie region, the eastern Czech portion of Cieszyn Silesia, was annexed by Poland.On March 14, 1939, the area was divided into the Protectorate of Bohemia and Moravia and the Slovak Republic, and for all intents and purposes, we were now Slovakian Jews.

The Hlinka's People's Party, with its anti-Jewish platform, was formed shortly thereafter, and the Hlinka Guard, our indigenous version of German Brownshirts, was soon terrorizing Jews across the Slovak Republic.

The new Slovak Republic quickly became a satellite of the Third Reich under the notorious Father Jozef Tiso. Within a month, anti-Jewish legislation was on the books, hateful slogans against the Jews were scrawled on walls around Piešťany, while antisemitism was promoted in newspapers and brought to life in acts of vandalism against our community.

In the summer of 1940, Adolf Eichmann's emissary, Dieter Wisliceny, arrived in Bratislava to advise the Slovak regime on how to oust Jews from the country's economy. My father's business was taken away and "sold" to a non-Jew. Then rocks flying through our front windows became a fact of life. The Pro Labora Hotel across the street became local Hlinka Guard headquarters, and young men coming to and from the hotel hurled stones and epithets our way just for the fun of it.

Papa realized there was no point in replacing the windows so, in disgust, he boarded them over. The apartment was no longer filled with sunlight and joy — it was dark and gloomy. Not long after that, Jews were no longer permitted to attend public schools. My brothers would come home from the Jewish school with bloodied clothes and bruises on their arms and faces. Nasty thugs stood around the streets — Jew-baiting, shouting curses at us, and more and more often made their points with fists and homemade weapons.

Turi was easily provoked and fought back, giving as good as he got. After a while, my parents, fearing for our lives, simply kept us home from school and off the streets. Someone once tried to break down the great double doors to our house, but the old wood withstood the attack. We were — for the moment — safely barricaded behind them. But the continued isolation inexorably forced us in on ourselves.

Our home became a fortress and a refuge. For me, home and courtyard were just the right size, but for my older siblings and my parents, the world shrank daily. My parents did not have the luxury of avoiding reality. No grown-up could. It was all they talked about, all they thought about. My paternal Uncle Toyvi Mannheimer, who had immigrated to Mandate Palestine, came to visit in 1938 and urged my parents to get out, to join him there.

Like many other European Jews, my parents would not hear of it. Piešťany was their home. Their families had lived in Europe for generations, and they had heard that life in the Holy Land was very difficult. Everything Mama and Papa knew and owned, their extended families and networks of friends, were all around them. How could they leave?

They clung to a hope that their skills and services were needed, that the anti-Jewish measures and antisemitism were just window-dressing to appease the right-wing and make a show for the radicals in Germany; that the Third Reich, the madmen who led it and their henchmen, the Hlinka Guard, couldn't possibly last.

My parents, like millions of their fellow Jews, expected some difficulties, and felt certain all would come right again—as it had come right a hundred times before in the history of the Jewish people. And so they stayed. But with each successive wave of restrictions, their worries grew and their options narrowed.

I wonder how afraid they were when they talked late at night while we children slept. It is so hard, now that we know the ending, to imagine what it must have been like for them to see their world coming apart one day at a time, as they absorbed blow after blow after blow, never knowing when the next one might fall and from whence it would come. I did learn that they and their friends wanted desperately to find a way to get to Hungary, a relatively benign refuge for Jews until March 1944.

Had we made it, with our Hungarian-born mother and relatives scattered in and around Budapest, it would have been something of a homecoming. But although the Hungarian border was little more than 65 miles away, it might as well have been on the moon. Restrictions on movement by Jews were absolute and rigorously enforced. Traveling for almost all Jews was forbidden.

In one respect we were very lucky. When I began to research this book, I was told that my father had hidden his money and spent it on our safety, saving for what he hoped would be our escape. He also began to sell his assets so that when the time came, he could buy our lives. Mama tried to save us, too, and worked very hard to make sure we would stay healthy. Bella remembers how she would force us to drink lots of milk, but also noticed that the stress had changed Mama, who now never smiled.

We rarely went out, and when we did it was important not to attract attention. One way to do that was to make sure we didn't look well-off. When we got new clothing, Mama took our outfits into the courtyard and rubbed them into the soil, often soaking my dresses in mud to make them look old or secondhand. New shoes underwent the same treatment. My mother would bury them in the courtyard overnight so they would appear scuffed and well-worn. To a little girl who loved new clothes, who delighted in pretty dresses and shiny shoes, this was distressing and inexplicable.

Shoes were my great love, especially shiny new ones that gleamed in the light and had that fresh, pungent leather smell. Before the holidays, I happily looked forward to taking my new shoes out of their box, trying them on, and setting them on the floor beside my bed, ready for me to slip into them first thing in the morning. I loved to show them off, and would pirouette for Mama and my sisters. But the war changed all that.

And so I was wonderfully surprised when Mama brought home a beautiful new pair of shoes for me. I don't know how she got them, but there they were. Lovely, lovely shoes—shiny black leather Mary Janes I wanted to wear immediately.

But then Mama took me into the courtyard, holding the shoe box in one hand and my hand in the other. She looked around, and when she found a spot she liked, took a spoon out of her apron pocket, went down on her knees and dug a hole. Why on earth would Mama dig a hole in the courtyard?

I stood there and watched as the hole became big enough to bury my new shoes. And when Mama took them out of the box and put them in the hole, covering them with dirt, I was thunderstruck.

Why did Mama bury my beautiful shoes? I couldn't understand, I shook her shoulder as she kneeled in the dirt and demanded my shoes back.

She tried to explain that she had to do it and that one day I would understand why. She told me I would get them back in the morning.

I heard the words, but I could not cope with my sense of loss. I wept for my buried shoes; I lay down on the spot where she'd buried them, clung to the soil, and cried. The deprivation caused me deep pain because those lovely shoes rightly belonged to me—in their pristine, beautiful, brand-new state.

Mama left me to my misery, and eventually I found my way back to my room. Dejected and sad, I went to bed.

The next day, Mama brought me back to the courtyard and took my shoes out of the dirt. When I saw how dirty they were, I got really angry and didn't want to wear them. But Mama told me. "Only now can you wear the shoes."

I was really stubborn. I refused, but Mama explained that if the neighbors noticed my bright new shoes, we could be in trouble with the law because we were not allowed to own "new" things. Mama also concluded that we should not keep anything of value under the terrible conditions we were living under, so she and Papa figured out how to safe-keep certain items that were part of our family legacy.

They buried our family treasures under the stone stairs leading to our door. There were jewels, silver, linens and other heirlooms. I knew nothing about this; I was too young. But my mother showed Bella, the oldest of us, the spot where she'd buried what was left of our valuables and told her that if anything should happen to the family, she should come back and dig in that spot.

Perhaps Mama sensed even then that she might not survive what was coming. I'll never know. What seems clear is that someone—maybe a maid or a tenant—saw or learned or guessed where my mother pointed, for after the war, when Bella went back to Piešťany, there was very little left to dig up. (She found my mother's *Sabbath* candlesticks, which she kept; Papa's *Kiddush* cup was given to me, and the spice box we used at the ceremony that concluded the *Sabbath* was given to Bubi. She also found the necklace my mother wore as a beauty queen and some hand-embroidered linens. All the other heirlooms were gone.)

In April 1941, the Slovak Hlinka regime, under the stewardship of Wisliceny and his minions, began looting Jewish businesses in earnest. Jewish businesses were liquidated en masse and soon Papa couldn't even work in his own store. Yet, as an expert in textiles and master of many languages, including German, he was considered essential to the overall economy. The government appointed him to work as a sales representative for a German textile factory, and gave him papers that exempted him from the normal restrictions on Jews. They also allowed him to travel extensively.

On September 9 of that year, however, the government posted 270 anti-Jewish edicts. Among other things, they defined Jews as a racial minority, required

Jews over the age of six to wear a yellow Star of David, and made us available for forced labor at a moment's notice. Every aspect of Jewish life was circumscribed: the times of day we could shop, the streets we could walk on, the hours of curfew. We were cut out of the life of our nation, prohibited from entering parks and playgrounds, stripped of all rights, of any appeal to a higher authority.

For Papa, those 270 laws — and particularly the requirement to wear the yellow star — restricted his so-called freedom. Travel he could, but he was constantly harassed and often beaten. Once, he told us, he was so tired that he fell asleep on the train. For their amusement, his fellow passengers let him sleep past his stop — a good joke to play on the Jew. Another time, a gang of hooligans refused to let him off the train. Every trip became a minefield; he never knew what form his victimization would take, only that he would surely be treated malevolently. As a consequence, ironically, he would often wear clothes that did not have the star sewn on them, risking his life even more.

Yellow stars were sewn onto almost every garment we owned, except for some of Papa's jackets and coats and my clothing (because I was underage). For my siblings and parents, daring to walk outside without the star was to tempt death from those who hated us most.

Despite the propaganda and the government incitement to hate Jews, small farmers, tenant farmers, and agricultural workers who made up the bulk of the population in and around Piešťany had been served well by the Mannheimer family. Papa had built up a reservoir of goodwill among his customers. Perhaps it was simply his manner, the winning personality that was so attractive to family, friends, and business associates. Perhaps it was because he was generous about extending credit and stocked the store with the very things the peasants needed or because he managed to find items for them that were hard to get. In any event, there was an open line of communication between many of them and my parents. And my parents made use of it, especially when they looked for ways to escape.

In the fall and winter of 1941, my father, wanted for being a rich Jew and possible activist, arranged for us to hide in a peasant farmhouse in one of the farming villages that dotted the countryside. For a great deal of money, the peasants made a place for us in the back of their farmhouse. Day and night we stayed completely hidden, almost like prisoners—sneaking outside sometimes for a bit of fresh air. But when company came to visit the peasants—and sometimes, company meant Hlinka soldiers—we hid in a small, concealed room, where we would remain as quiet as we could until they left. These visits could sometimes last for hours, and for a youngster like me, staying quiet for so long was torture, especially if I had to go to the bathroom.

One bright day in early fall, as the leaves on the oak trees were turning gold and red, we heard engines approaching from the distance. We quickly scurried into our tiny, dark hiding place as a truck filled with Hlinka soldiers looking for Jews and food approached. The officers in charge soon banged on the house door while their troops loitered in a field outside, smoking cigarettes and chatting.

The peasants knew that the situation was dangerous for them and for us. If we were caught, we would all be killed, no exceptions. They had to make these Nazis feel welcome, and took the edge off the menace by inviting the officers in for vodka and beer. Soon the drinking led to laughter and the "social" call went on for a very long time until I could no longer ignore my urgent need to relieve myself.

I was adamant about not wetting myself and wanted to use the indoor toilet. But my parents were afraid that if I left the room, the soldiers would notice me, and I would be called over to entertain them because I was so cute. They were afraid I might say the wrong thing and arouse their suspicions. I was too young to know the difference between what was dangerous to say and not.

Mama finally decided I could take a risk and sneak out the back door to use the workers' privy on the other side of the barnyard. She felt no one would notice another peasant child—a fair-haired one at that—going back and forth across the yard to use the privy.

The outhouse was a wooden shed beyond the barn. In a practice that appalls us today, it was situated over a stream, so that the current would continually wash the sewage away. The distance between the house and the shed seemed huge, but I was determined to get there. I quickly scooted through the grass, keeping my head down, and made it to the privy door in record time.

I was alone—a small, skinny child barely able to reach the wooden bar that acted as the door handle. I stood on tiptoe as I reached up to pull it open, and stepped up onto a platform that formed the floor of the outhouse. The smell inside was foul; I almost threw up.

The "toilet" was a hole in the floor with a wall of crudely nailed together planks in front of it, and another plank nailed flat across the top to form a narrow shelf-edge, a "seat" over the opening. That "wall" came up to my shoulders, forcing me to climb it to get to the "seat."

I struggled to get to the top and tried to turn around so I could sit forward, but lost my balance and fell backwards into the opening. Panic-stricken, I found myself caught in a repellent underground current of sewage that was intent on pulling me down. I tried to scream, but, at first, nothing came out of my mouth.

For a fastidious child like me, this was a horrifying nightmare come true. The filth, the darkness, relieved only by stray sunbeams struggling in between the planks of the privy walls, terrified me. The foul current pulled at me, dragging me into a loathsome undertow of the blackest waste. I finally wrenched out a high-pitched scream from the depths of my being, but no one could hear it. I choked, my throat frozen, my body wracked by spasms. My fear was intense, scarier and more dreadful than the fear of the flying rocks that came through our windows in Pieštany.

I sensed that if I did not help myself, I would be lost, literally forever. I would drown in that fetid stink-hole. I reached up, clutching at air, my hand flailing for something to grab onto. Every time I thought I could grab a plank with my thin fingers, I lost my grip because it was slippery with stinking slime.

I fell back into the muck and reached up again. Again, I fell. And again. And again. I was struggling hard now, hurling my arm up, kicking and scratching against the current, reaching for something, anything, to grip. Screaming my dry, soundless scream, I felt myself being swallowed as if by quicksand and wondered if I would ever get out.

Then, quite suddenly, I felt my arm being lifted. In the dim, gray light, I spotted a nail sticking out of the slick, slimy wall. I reached up and grabbed it as if it were waiting for me. I clutched it and held on for dear life as the vile current continued to swirl around me, covering me from head to toe. And then I began to climb, going from one nail to another and then another. The nails were rusty and bloodied my fingers, but I never felt the pain, for it was truly as if someone was there helping me—some ineffable presence, some source of strength well beyond my own. Reach up, grab a nail, place the foot in a crack or on a nail, climb, reach again, climb some more.

I remember thinking: "I have to survive! I cannot die in this filth. I must live! I will live!"

Finally I succeeded in hauling myself to the top of the latrine wall. I flipped my body over the edge of the opening and knew I was safe. Shaking, I stood up and opened the door to breathe in the fresh air, crying with fear and relief and not knowing whether I should be happy or miserable.

So powerful is this memory — the fall into the abyss, the terror, the struggle, the sudden lifting embrace, as it seemed, from some unknown source — that to think of it is to be transported back to that time and place. I can still feel how my hands grasped each nail. I can still feel my feet climbing that wall, nail by nail, and my throat becomes tight.

And then I thank God, for I truly believe it was God's hand that reached down that day to lift my arm and my hope, my faith, and my determination. I am convinced God's hand guided my own to the nails that served as my ladder to life.

During the epic struggle to save myself, I had wished, in vain, that someone would be waiting for me outside the privy door. There was no one in sight, except Hlinka soldiers who were still lolling about. I quickly made my way to the barn and stayed hidden in the hayloft until they left. Perhaps Mama had silently prayed for me to find a hiding place and to remain there. I didn't know. But if she did, her prayer was answered. I stank and shivered as I wondered when I could get to Mama and feel safe in her arms. Finally the Hlinka soldiers left, the yard was empty, and the house was quiet.

I dashed out of the barn as if it was on fire and stumbled across the yard. Mama saw me and came running. She understood at once what had happened and that she had almost lost me. She hugged me tightly to her despite the stinking muck that covered me. Then she and the peasants took me to the water pump and washed me off, scrubbing me until I turned pink. They rubbed me down with fragrant scents, and after a while I looked like a little girl again. But I was no longer the same little girl I had been that morning. I had faced death and inspired by God managed to save my own life, with my own resources, through my fiercely indomitable will to live. When I look back at that day, I realize I was just a small slip of a thing. But I had done it.

God touched me that day and drew me back from the brink, providing me with the needed will to live and the promise He would never let me go, that He would watch over me forever. My encounter proved that there is strength of will that keeps those who have hope and faith alive.

After that, my parents never let me out of their sight. Even so, a few months later, we were asked to leave the farm. The peasants were afraid a similar incident at the wrong time could tip off the Hlinka. It didn't matter, anyway. In the spring of 1942, all the Jews of Piešťany were ordered to report to the main square, with their luggage, for deportation to Žilina.

Chapter Three
Betrayal and Deportation

Spring comes late to Slovakia. It was a cloudy, cool day with just a hint of rain in the air when the peasants who sheltered us told us we had to leave. In March 1942, the population had gotten one last warning from the Hlinka Guard against harboring Jews and, by the look of things, they complied en masse. As we left our hideaway, the eight of us joined a slow march of Jews who made their way, as ordered, to the Piešťany town square. It was the first of many roundups I was to live through.

When we arrived in Piešťany, our town looked much as it had before we fled, but something fundamental had changed. My family and all the Jewish citizens had become strangers in our hometown. Our neighbors looked at us with contempt instead of respect.

Our line snaked through familiar streets. Young and old clutched the few possessions they could manage: luggage, huge bundles tied onto backs and held under arms, suitcases, satchels — even buckets — were loaded with clothing, household goods, heirlooms, anything of value.

In the square, not far from the fountain where I once drank the bitter waters, there was no sugar now to sweeten our lives. Although we did not know it at the time, 1942 was the beginning of the end, the moment when the shadow of death fell over us, when the Nazis, meeting in the Berlin suburb of Wannsee, made the decision to put the death machine into motion and solve the *Jewish problem*.

While the Jews of Pieštany "celebrated" the first Passover Seder on Wednesday evening, April 1, 1942, 1,000 Jewish girls were deported to Auschwitz, among them 50 girls from Pieštany. That was the last Seder our family spent together.

The heart of the torture was the round up, the roll call—the endless count, the infinitely long wait to check the lists of Jews as we stood there, hour after hour, rain or shine. That first roundup would not be the last time that we would be made to feel like herd animals.

Žilina.

That day, once they were satisfied with the count, the secret police and the Hlinka Guard packed us tightly onto open trucks and shipped us 73 miles northwest to Žilina, a town in a corner of Slovakia that had long been a trading and transportation hub. That spring and summer, Jews were the main commodities loaded into freight wagons—nearly 60,000 of us, three-quarters of all the Jews in Slovakia. And when we got to Žilina, they corralled us into a transit camp, a *Lager*, an old army barracks where the Jews of Pieštany and surrounding towns and villages were to "live" in captivity until deportation to the East, to Poland, to God-knows-where.

Each barrack housed about a hundred people, who were forced to sleep on wooden bunks with thin, lice-infested straw mattresses. There was no privacy and few facilities for sanitation or hygiene. The transit camp was a place of numbers—roll call numbers, numbers tacked onto our clothing or scrawled across the backs of our coats, numbers shouted out by the Hlinka Guards. Everyone had a number; everyone was counted. During the day, children were separated

The *Lager* in Žilina.

from their parents, who were taken to work in labor brigades. And each week, some of those people were counted out and climbed into a cattle car to head for that place no one spoke of or dared think about. (The Germans greeted these trains at their border and took over the passengers' fates.)

The *Lager* was fenced-in by barbed wire and filled with overwhelming numbers of people. Soldiers and Hlinka Guards patrolled the perimeter; the underlying sense of menace was claustrophobic. For the Germans, who were paid by the Slovakians to rid them of their Jews, each weekly transport meant another quota was successfully filled, another thousand Jews subtracted. By the late spring and early summer of 1942, some deportees had escaped from Poland's death camps and brought word of what was happening to a few trusted members of the Jewish Office, the *Ústredna Židov*, our equivalent of the *Jüdenrat*. Whether my parents heard this news—breathtaking in its horror and surpassing all understanding—and whether they believed it, I will never know.

Some Jews were exempt from deportation. These included those who converted to Christianity, Jews married to non-Jews and individuals considered essential to the social or economic life of the country. Such exemptions were extended to the individual's spouse and children as well. Papa managed to obtain such papers when the factory he represented intervened with the authorities. A so-called certificate of exemption was duly issued and before our number was called, we were allowed to leave the camp. Still, we had to remain in Žilina, and my father had to report to the authorities as ordered. He found us an apartment in town and, for me at least, the world returned to a semblance of normalcy.

Papa's exemption meant that we didn't have to go to the roundups. We were also able to sleep on beds and be together at "home." We lived quietly, trying to become invisible.

As part of a normal routine, I was allowed to play with non-Jewish children. At that age, of course, children don't question the ethnic or religious backgrounds of their playmates; they haven't yet been taught to hate. And my own parents seemed unworried about my "mingling." Perhaps they hoped it would blind our neighbors to the fact that we were Jews— exempt Jews, but Jews nonetheless.

Gone, however, were the fine garments of Piešťany, or the care my mother took to make sure we all looked "just so" before we ventured outdoors. My worn clothes looked authentic because they were indeed threadbare. Little attention was paid to a blouse not tightly tucked into a skirt, or hair not perfectly combed. Things that once bothered Mama were no longer important.

The strict observance of our faith, the ritual that once regulated each action of each day of our lives, was abandoned in order not to draw attention to ourselves as Jews. We lived like moles, burrowing deeper and deeper underground. My family ripped the yellow Stars of David from our clothing and learned to live as non-Jews. My mother gave up the head covering she routinely wore. What suffered most was *Shabbat*.

The peace was gone. Our ritual was conducted in whispers—without candles, without challah, without wine. Mama taught us to light the candles in our hearts. We might disguise who we were, but we never denied our faith.

But no Jew could be completely invisible in the world of the Hlinka Guard and their friends, the Nazis, so when my father's exemption was cancelled a month or two later, we fled. I don't know how it was managed, but we left Žilina and went to Bratislava.

The Jews of Bratislava had been expelled more than a year earlier to peripheral towns and labor camps hastily constructed to receive them. The consequences of this expulsion were as yet unknown, but to my desperate parents it meant there was empty living space to be had in Bratislava. We found an apartment and settled in, but just a few days later our neighbors noticed the "new" tenants in what should have been an empty apartment. One day they approached my father and asked him who he was and what he was doing there.

Papa wasted no time. We picked up our bundles and moved again. Another empty Jewish apartment was found and we moved in. When neighbors began asking questions a few days later, we moved again. It became a pattern. Whenever the least danger was sensed, we left the building we were in. There was no hesitation, no discussion, and no analysis of what might happen if we did this or that or the other. As easy prey for the hunters, our only hope was to stay at least one step ahead of them.

We were always on the move. Sometimes that meant staying in a different hiding place each night. Sometimes, we could stay a few days. I think Papa must have been a magician to keep us out of the clutches of the secret police for such a long time. And I believe he thought he would succeed in getting us through the war. His primary concern was to protect us.

Of course, he had money, and that certainly helped. But he must have been tremendously resourceful. I don't remember how many times we moved. I was always with my parents, always in the bosom of the family, always the coddled one. I was where I belonged, in my parents' arms.

Papa, with his tall stature and reddish-blond hair, did not look like the typical Jew. He could have been any successful German-Slovak businessman traveling on business essential to the Reich. Clever, engaging, educated, fluent in several languages, he made it his business to find out what was going on, and perhaps that is why he always managed to keep our family one step ahead of the enemy.

That summer a few Jewish activists formed an underground Working Group, the *Pracovná Skupina,* the "other government." It was led by Gisi Fleischmann, once the head of the Women's International Zionist Organization and by Rabbi Micheol Ber Weissmandl, son-in-law of Rabbi Ungar, who had been the head of the yeshiva funded by my Aunt Giska and Uncle Simon Katscher in the town of Nitra. The ultra-Orthodox Ungar and the Zionist Fleischmann were cousins from different ends of the spectrum of Jewish life, but she and his son-in-law Weissmandl banded together to save Jews. The underground group they formed was determined to stop the deportations and was later recognized for saving more than 30,000 Jews during the Holocaust. Giska and Simon were involved with them.

By mid-1942, Slovak public opinion, mostly indifferent when the deportations first began, turned against indigenous antisemitism. Church leaders spoke against "excessive bigotry," though what mostly concerned them was the maltreatment of Jewish converts to Catholicism. But when the Slovak regime began to slow down the deportations, their reasons were hardly humanitarian. These officials were more interested in the money they could "earn" by selling emigration permits to wealthy Jews.

Did Papa hope to obtain such an emigration permit? Did he contribute money for bribes for Adolf Eichmann's deputy, Dieter Wisliceny? Eichmann was Hitler's notorious henchman and the "manager" of Holocaust logistics. I will never know what really happened. But what is known is that in the summer of 1942, the deportations slowed.

At the time, we lived in a nice apartment in a nice building in Žilina. I remember playing with neighbors' children and that my brothers went to school. But the peaceful interlude did not last.

One day, Hlinka Guardsmen confronted my father on a train and threatened to arrest him. Papa, as nimble-witted as he was personable, somehow managed to talk his way out of it. He found another temporary refuge and got word to us to come there so the family could be together. Papa paid a fortune for the apartment and for forged Aryan documents he had somehow managed to obtain. That August, no transports left Slovakia. The word was out that the authorities were no longer scheduling deportations. Instead, a transport was to be dispatched only when a group of 1,000 Jews could be gathered at one of the concentration centers.

But then Eichmann arrived in town near the end of August. He immediately ordered one transport of Jews per week to be deported and commanded a crackdown on the number of exemptions. The Hlinka government quickly complied and demanded that every agency review Jewish documents — certificates of exemption, letters of protection, and work permits. The reviews went slowly, and with Wisliceny and others willing to wait while the *Pracovná Skupina* struggled to meet their demands for bribes, there was no rush to round up Jews. But the Tuka-Mach, an anti-Semitic group named for Prime Minister Vojtech Tuka and Alexander Mach, the leader of the Hlinka Guard, deplored the slowdown and decreed each transport must contain 1,000 Jews, setting off a hunt for every Jew they could find. People were offered incentives to turn in their neighbors and friends — and it worked.

September arrived and the High Holy Days came and went. I do not remember the details. Did Papa pray? Did Mama light candles and prepare any type of special foods? Did Papa bless us? If Papa were caught with a prayer book, his life would have been forfeit. If Mama lit candles, she would have risked our very lives. Try as I might, it becomes painfully impossible to recall what happened on the last High Holidays we spent as a family. What I do remember is the luxurious warmth and love from the times we celebrated on Štefaniková Street, and I thought I would never experience anything like that again.

Hunkered down in our high-priced refuge, could my parents have dared to hope that they had found safety? By mid-September, the government authorities collected enough Jews for two more transports to Poland. When the deportations were again stopped for lack of "cargo," the Tuka-Mach sweetened the pot by offering bounties for the head of each Jew turned over to them. As September gave way to October, Jews became hot commodities worth a considerable amount of money to those willing to ferret out and consign them to an abysmal fate.

Papa thought that those who provided him with the apartment and papers would honor the deal, but they betrayed us. Our safety had been purchased at inflated prices that only the wicked would demand and only the desperate would pay, but I cannot say when the betrayal took place. I came to my conclusion over the years by listening to older Slovakian survivors tell their stories, by talking to relatives and reading books. I do not know who turned us in. Perhaps it was a greedy landlord or someone who wanted the apartment. What is certain is that the people my father paid and trusted, those whose loyalty he'd relied on, handed us over.

It happened on a crisp October day. I was at home with my parents, playing with an old toy on the wooden living room floor. Bella, Bubi and Turi were in school for the day. Rena and Robi were at half-day school and were expected home for lunch. Then one of them would take me to my afternoon nursery class.

Mama was busy with her sewing basket, darning socks. She kept checking to see if I was all right, and would smile at me occasionally. Papa was reading his newspaper. It was quiet and peaceful.

Suddenly we heard the urgent clatter of military boots on the stone stairs. It stopped right in front of our apartment door. Then the pounding, loud and insistent, began. Mama turned pale and opened the door to admit two imposing men who stood before us in their gray and black uniforms. I was at eye level with their boots — high, polished, black boots that tightly encased their feet and calves up to their knees. My gaze continued upward, tracing belted tunics, leather gloves, strange lightning markings on their uniforms and hats. They were soldiers. I recognized them as the enemy we constantly tried to flee, and I was terrified. In Slovakia in the early 1940s you learned to distinguish between police, the Hlinka Guard, regular soldiers and the secret service.

They did not smile. They disdained small courtesies. They were impatient. They wanted to see Papa and our papers — without delay. Papa came into the room to talk to them and was deferential and polite. He introduced Mama and me to the officers. I could see my reflection in their shiny boots, but I was afraid to raise my eyes to their faces.

I sensed this was trouble, big trouble. I held my breath. Not for a second did I doubt Papa would save the day, that he would get us through this as he had done so many times before. I could hear my own heart beating with anxiety, but I knew he would protect us once again.

Papa brought out the papers and handed them over. "I think you'll find everything in order," he said.

The papers must have been very well executed forgeries. The ranking officer examined them. Then he handed them to his fellow officer. Back and forth the papers went as the two of them exchanged glances, as if deciding what to do.

Then the ranking officer shook his head. "Something doesn't look right," he said. "We will take the papers to headquarters for closer examination and return them to you later."

My father protested, politely insistent. "How long will you be? The papers are our proof of identity. If someone else should come and demand the papers...."

His arguments were dismissed out of hand. The officer sternly replied "Don't worry. We'll bring the papers back later." Then they stomped out, taking our lifeline—the hard-won, costly papers that identified us as Aryans—with them.

I cannot begin to imagine what went through my parents' minds that morning. We were exposed, our papers in the hands of the dreaded secret police. The three children in school and the two others were due to come home at any moment. Did my parents think of escaping? Without papers, where could they go? Perhaps Papa thought that he could once more talk or bribe our way out of trouble. He had managed to keep us alive and safe so many times before; there was no reason he shouldn't manage it again.

After the secret police left, I blithely continued to play, oblivious to the danger, and paid no attention to my parents' worried whispers. Rena and Robi came home from school and we all had lunch. Our parents didn't want us to sense there was a problem, so they acted as if everything was normal. Then Papa dropped me off at my nursery school and went back to the apartment.

An hour or two later, the secret police returned to the apartment with additional men and found the four of them there. Mama was doing the mending, Papa was reading the paper, and my siblings were doing their homework. Neighbors watched as my parents, Rena, and Robi were taken to the *Lager* in Žilina.

People immediately went to the school and collected Bubi, Turi and Bella, and told them that the rest of the family, except for me, was taken. I remember that it was a gray, cloudy day. I was in the school yard playing hide-and-seek with my classmates when I noticed that someone was talking to my sister and brothers. Then I saw them crying, so I went to my teacher and asked why they were crying and if I could join them. The teacher took my hand and brought me over. She bent down and told me that our parents and siblings had been taken, that they were gone, and that we had to be strong because we were now alone.

I can still see Bella, Bubi and Turi leaning against a tree as if it was holding them up while they sobbed inconsolably. I wept, too, but without understanding exactly why. I was scared, but still expected my parents to come back. This was all confusing and beyond my comprehension. My parents had been my only reality, my sisters and brothers were my anchors.

The people in the underground did not mince words. They were direct with us and didn't try to sweeten the truth. When the secret police went back to the apartment, they thought they would find a family of eight—the number of names that appeared on their papers. Because the arresting officers found only four family members in the apartment, the Slovak regime declared that we four Mannheimer children were dangerous fugitives wanted for the heinous crime of being Jewish.

The people who took us in told us we were in serious danger and had to do exactly as we were told. We couldn't make scenes, throw temper tantrums, or behave like normal children. We were being hunted like animals, and we had to help those who wanted to save us by listening and doing exactly as instructed. We were to stay quiet and behave like grownups.

The members of Weissmandl and Fleischmann's working group took care of us from the moment they fetched us from our schools—and even after almost everyone had been deported or executed, the group continued to rescue Jews.

Who were these people? Some were trusted members of the government-sanctioned Jewish Office. Others had relatives or connections with ways of helping. My sister and brothers and I never could figure out how they managed to do what they did on our behalf—or why. But during the following hectic days, we were separated and moved from place to place, from family to family. The Slovaks were looking for a group of four children, under the mistaken assumption that our rescuers would keep us together.

By separating us, the committee saved our lives. I didn't see Bella and Turi for weeks, and I missed them. Someone had arranged to have them taken to my Aunt Giska in Vicsáp, an estate in the countryside near Nitra, about 50 miles northeast of Bratislava.

Because agriculture was essential to the economy, and because Jewish-run farms tended to be well-organized and well-mechanized, Aryanization of such farms was discouraged. My Uncle Simon was thus exempted from deportation. Bella and Turi were safe there for quite some time—not in my aunt's house, but hidden on the estate, which was really a village. There they blended into the company of the peasants and their children.

I don't know where I was taken, but I was soon reunited with Bubi in Žilina. We remained together after that. I have no memory of the people who took charge of us, moved us, hid us and cared for us, but by separating us they were able to keep the four of us alive. They also brought us a message from Papa: Under no circumstances were we to come to the Žilina *Lager*. He was worried that we would try to join him and Mama.

Soon word was out: A transport would be leaving Žilina for Poland on October 20, 1942, and our parents, Rena and Robi would be on it. The event was presented as a public "picnic" to attract crowds. I later learned that this doublespeak was one method the Slovaks and their collaborators used to persuade people to come out of hiding and give themselves up.

There were many people who of their own free will decided to join the rest of their families in the *Lager*. They did not know they were headed for certain death, and my father's greatest fear was that in our need for him and Mama we would be tempted to come to the gates. If we did, he knew we would be doomed. He understood that anyone was vulnerable; the secret police and Hlinka Guard picked up any Jews they could find to make Eichmann's quota of 1,000 Jews per train.

Though we didn't go to the *Lager*, on October 20 Bubi and I decided to go to the railway station to watch what was happening. Together we agreed that if we could, we would join our parents, Rena and Robi on their journey.

There was a large crowd near the platform, and it included many Jews filled with despair who asked to enter the cattle cars with their husbands or wives, parents, children, brothers or sisters. To them, it must have seemed the only choice—to be with the people you loved, no matter what fate had in mind. They seemed almost eager to walk into the maw of hell itself.

For the locals, this day was indeed a picnic—a festive diversion. They came to celebrate and watch the Jews of Slovakia disappear forever.

I stood near the platform, clutching Bubi's hand in the midst of that ogling, exuberant crowd. At the Žilina train station, Bubi and I—two scrawny kids—stood trembling in the midst of the yelling mob. We could hear the thwacks of the sticks beating against Jewish flesh and the approving murmurs from the crowd around us. We strained our necks and stood on our toes as we looked for our parents. From that moment on, I could not bear to let go of Bubi's hand. The noise— the shouts, the beatings, all the vicious activity—was overwhelming. My knees were giving way, and I clung all the closer to my brother.

I remember counting lots and lots of cattle cars. Some of them were for animals and freight. The rest were marked with the letter Z. Only later did I learn that Z stood for *Židov*—Jews. Crude wooden ramps were placed at the opening of each car. Near the end of the railroad platform, several desks were set up in a row. Behind each one sat a Hlinka Guardsman with

Deportation from Žilina (*courtesy Yad Vashem*).

a list. In lines kept straight by guards with rifles and policemen with cudgels, the Jews from the Žilina *Lager* passed by these desks as their names were checked off. Then they were herded up the ramps into the cattle cars, packed in as tightly as possible.

The Jews who cowered in these lines were swaddled in layers of clothing, and all carried bundles. Yellow Stars of David that had incorporated the word *Jude* in its center were sewn on the fronts and backs of their threadbare apparel. Officials ticked their names off in front of the cattle cars that took them away. Some women wore kerchiefs or hats; some men and boys wore caps that once were jaunty. Even children carried their own belongings. They stared at the cameras present, their faces grim, the light gone out of their eyes. You could sense that life was already gone from their souls. They looked powerless and confused. Despair bent their backs, as their humanity was reduced, pared down by a hatred of unprecedented barbarity. They were lost, and they knew they were lost forever. Even a little girl like me saw their hopelessness on that day.

"Faster! Faster!" the persecutors shouted at their bereft passengers. Orders and insults were barked out; the very old, the very young, even the very sick, were treated with contempt. Beatings continued to accompany the shouts; a cudgel was repeatedly whipped across the back or face or legs of someone who did not move fast enough.

There was method to this madness. The aim was to create an environment of tension, fear, and despair. To add insult to injury, and to complete their humiliation, the Jews were forced to pay for their passage and for "damages" to the cattle cars.

The Hlinka Guards knew how to psychologically terrorize their captives. The Nazis took over the trains at the Slovak-German border. By the time their hapless victims arrived in Auschwitz, almost all of them were incapable of resisting their fate. The long lines, the constant shouting, the physical torture and, above all, the crowded and hellish cattle cars with standing room only, with no light and little air and just a bucket for everyone's slops, all were part of the nefarious scheme to destroy a people.

The long train idled in the station, with black smoke spewing from its stacks. It was a dark, morbid sight that gave me the chills. Suddenly, through the haze, we saw Mama, Papa, Robi and Rena pass the last checkpoint and how they were pushed and shoved up a ramp into a cattle car. I began to scream. I began to sob. I wanted my Mama. I wanted my Papa. I wanted Rena and Robi back with me, to play with me, to be with me. I wanted us all back together as a family. I wanted the safety I had always known in the warm bosom of my family. I wanted the peace and protection I used to find in my father's embrace.

Why was all of this happening? What was I doing in this awful world? I didn't stop screaming. Suddenly Papa caught sight of us, and his face turned ashen with fear. "Go away!" he shouted at Bubi and me. "Do not get on this train. Go away!"

Papa surely knew where they were going and ordered us to disappear. Later, we learned that Papa, still useful to the regime, had been offered a chance to get off the train. This time, however, the exemption was for him alone — without his wife and children. He refused to leave them. He wouldn't let Mama, Rena and Robi take the final journey alone.

When he saw Bubi and me in the crowd, he understood he had thus far saved four of his children; there was a chance we might live. That's what he was thinking when he shouted for us to leave, to flee. "Live! Choose life!" he yelled at us from a distance. "Survive! Nothing else matters. Go and live!"

Out of the corner of my eye, I could see a Hlinka guard checking us out. Still, I could not stop screaming. I could not stop sobbing. "Mama!" I cried, "Mama! Mama! Papa! Don't leave me! Don't leave me! Take me with you! Please take me with you!"

The guard walked over to us and pointed the barrel of his rifle at my head. The point of his bayonet was an inch from my eye. "If you don't stop screaming," he snarled, "I'll throw you on that train. I am sure you would like that!" and started to laugh maniacally.

I instantly became as silent as stone. More importantly, I became as silent as Papa wanted me to be. With the bayonet in my face, I suddenly felt that same urge for life I felt when I was drowning in the filthy stream under the privy at the peasant's house. The instinct for survival surfaced in me once more. Dazed with confusion, my heart breaking with loss, terrified of the future, as young as I was, I understood that I wanted to live. Papa had done so much to try to keep us all alive. Even in that very last moment, the last time my brother and I were ever to see him, he bravely and nobly urged life upon us.

I remained silent while the heavy cattle car doors were slammed shut and locked from the outside—locking in despair and sadness, misery and pain. My Mama and Papa were gone with my brother Robi and sister Rena. I silently watched as the remaining cattle cars were loaded and as their doors were slammed shut and locked. I remained silent as Bubi and I searched for our family's faces but saw only the faces of strangers pressed against the sides of the cattle cars, their hands waving pitifully through the slats as black smoke from the stacks cast a menacing cloud over the station. I was silent as the train grunted into gear and began moving slowly away, while the vicious mob around us cheered and applauded. And I remained silent until all there was left to see was a wisp of gray smoke as the train headed north into Poland, which I later learned went to Oswiecim, to Auschwitz.

The day I lost my parents was the day my childhood abruptly ended. Life stopped when the train pulled away, taking with it, I thought, the very core of me. I hoped that my parents would come back and get me. This was my fantasy, one I held on to well into my teenage years, for I simply could not grasp the concept of never, ever, seeing my parents again.

I was too young to understand the finality of death, but I was not too young to feel abandoned and lost. I was not too young to know that my "security blanket" was gone, that the loving and protective shelter my parents had constructed around me was shattered.

There was no certainty in my life anymore—and no safety anywhere. And I didn't even know how or when they died.

In 2000, Bubi obtained a copy of a document labeled, in a florid European hand-writing, "Žilina, XXVIII Transport, Abgang 20.X.1942." It is a precisely typewritten list of names of the people in the eleventh car of that last transport. The page was stamped by the *Ustredna Židov*, the Jewish Office of Žilina and bears the heading "Žilina-Sillein." Further identifiers are "XXVIII Transport, 11th cata-Zug," Czech and German for "train." The *Ordner* (foreman) for the car is listed as Gartner, Leopold. Forty-five names are on the list, all of them checked off by hand as each deportee was herded onto the train.

Numbers 40 through 43 on the list, also from Pieštany, are my family, although the name is spelled "Manheim" and the birthdates of my sister and brother are wrongly given. Eugen Mannheimer, age 47; Dora Ungar Mannheimer, age 37; Rena Mannheimer, age 8; and Robi Mannheimer, age 7—murdered by the Nazis in Auschwitz in 1942 and lost forever to those who remained behind.

I learned that the train that took my parents and my older siblings to Auschwitz was the last transport of Jews—1100 of them—from Žilina. Transport XXVIII arrived in Auschwitz on October 21, 1942. Of the 1100 Žilina Jews taken that day, only 302 were selected for work duty. Since the Birkenau death factory associated with Auschwitz was still under construction, the other 798 men, women and children were herded immediately to Auschwitz I and killed there.

Whether my family met death on arrival at the camp or survived for a few weeks, months or even years, I do not know. I do know it is almost impossible for me to read accounts of deportations, selections and murder. It is impossible for me to look at the films and photographs of those events, for I can see and hear what was happening all too clearly. It happened to my family, as it happened to millions—the vast numbers are incomprehensible. Yet each one of those millions was a life, precious and unique.

CHAPTER FOUR
Walk to Hungary

We were four orphans—the Mannheimer gang of child fugitives, aged 4 through 13—running and hiding from the huge killing machine created by the Nazis and their collaborators. My memories of that time are solidly locked in a vault tightly sealed by trauma, resisting the chisel of remembrance. Separated from the others, I rely on Bubi's memories to fill those weeks.

It was late autumn, 1942—the beginning of November—not long after I saw my family being deported on that God-forsaken train. The Working Group kept Bubi and me together. Bella and Turi were separated from us and from each other. We didn't know where they were. It was now weeks since the Slovak secret police had pounded on our apartment door and the "four Mannheimer children" were turned into wanted criminals. They hadn't figured out that we were no longer together. Our rescuers continued to keep us separated and in motion. Bubi and I were always moved after dark, shifted from one farm to another, from one family to another. I do not know—will never know—how these havens were paid for, whether family or friends of my parents or members of the Working Committee had access to my family's assets or if we were dependent on the kindness of strangers.

After weeks of being shuffled around the countryside, we were brought back to Žilina. Bubi was assigned menial jobs in a bakery—errand boy, water boy, janitor; he did whatever they asked him to do and I never left his side. I adamantly refused to be separated from him for even a nano-second and literally held onto him even as he carried out his chores. There was no time for play, and there was certainly no school to attend. Our lives were spent trying to make it through each day, moment by moment. We were on our own, until someone managed to get word to our Aunt Giska at her estate near Nitra.

As the crow flies, the distance between Žilina and Nitra is about 70 miles. But the western curve of the arch formed by the Carpathian Mountains sits between the two towns, and getting over the mountains in 1942, with war and cataclysm convulsing the area, made it difficult to communicate. It took some time before Aunt Giska learned that Bubi and I were back in Žilina, but as soon as she heard, she dispatched someone trustworthy to claim us and bring us to the estate.

I don't remember the person who led us over the mountains to Giska—what he looked like, how he acted, whether he was tall or short, gruff or kindly. He must have been resourceful, brave, and clever to succeed in getting us over the mountains and down into the fertile plain of Nitra. He saved our lives, and for that I am grateful. But when we arrived in Nitra, Bella and Turi weren't

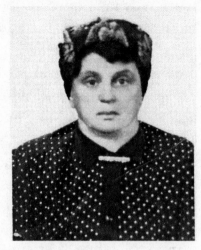

My savior, Aunt Giska.

there. I had no idea they were in hiding.

When Bubi and I arrived we were enveloped in the warm hugs and family we desperately needed after weeks on the run. I realized that there was someone in this place who genuinely cared for us. But I soon realized those hugs were rare. Aunt Giska was very much the matriarch—completely in control of the family—one that now clearly included Bubi and me. I knew little about her. She was considerably older than my father—the oldest sister and second oldest sibling in the family—and seemed to me elderly and distant. Her children were my parents' age; her grandchildren were my contemporaries.

Yet I liked what I saw. She looked like a queen: tall, straight-backed and solid, dressed in ankle-length black dresses topped by a snowy white apron embellished with a fine gold brooch. Her long black dresses were of the finest fabrics and the crocheted shawl she always wore was fashioned by her own hands. She covered her hair as required by Jewish tradition, and on *Shabbat* she wore gold bracelets encrusted with precious gems and small pearl earrings.

She carried herself with dignity and ran the estate and the household like an English squire who knows his business and his peasants. As well as caring for the estate, Aunt Giska was a wonderful cook, a great baker, and an expert at sewing, knitting and tatting. Every table was covered in lace tablecloths; lace anti-macassars covered the sofas. (An anti-macassar is a piece of fabric that protects chairs and sofas from the hair tonics that were used in the old days. Today these doilies, as we call them, are purely decorative.) There were lace mats on every table and under every knick-knack. There were jewel-toned area rugs in every room and a cheery fire was always burning in the hearth. The kitchen always smelled delicious because something wonderful was always simmering on the stove or baking in the oven. Best of all there were always raspberry-filled Linzer torts for us to nosh. Later, I came to appreciate Giska's fastidious ways and to understand her insistence on having the very best of everything.

Though Giska tried as hard as she could to offer us stability and security, we knew the feeling of safe harbor was delusional. If, in their relentless search, the secret police found us on Giska's estate, she and her family would be lost as well. At any moment the authorities could call for a raid of her properties and conduct one of their sadistic and thorough searches for loot, food, or hidden refugees. When friendly and loyal peasants were able to warn Giska, we were hidden in their haylofts and barns. But as the war heated up and the danger to the Jews in Slovakia grew inexorably, we understood that it wouldn't be long before we would have to run again. We played for time while Giska made arrangements for us to leave the only country we had ever known.

The plan was to get us into Hungary, Germany's ally since 1940. The deal the Hungarians had made with Germany was that Hitler would give them territorial concessions and leave them alone as long as they intensified their antisemitic measures. Later I learned that until March 1944, the Hungarians managed to resist the worst excesses of Nazi anti-Jewish policy and Hungary remained a haven for Slovakian Jews and other Jewish refugees from Eastern and Central Europe.

Giska had another reason to send us to Hungary. We had close relatives there: my maternal grandparents, aunts and uncles all lived in Hungary; another paternal aunt, Mela Itcskovitz, wife of Ferri, a wealthy car dealer, lived in Békéscsaba; my mother's oldest sister, Margit Katz, lived with her husband Jeno and their four children in Budapest. Turi and Bella were placed with families near the estate, and Bubi and I were to be smuggled, one hiding place at a time, to our Aunt Margit in Budapest.

Perhaps the people who were bringing us to Hungary were heirs to a long smuggling tradition, professionals who simply replaced last year's alcohol, jewels, or tobacco for the current most popularly traded item—Jews. Perhaps they were new to the game, finding profit, as people do, in the tragedies of others. They might even have been partisans or political dissidents who risked their lives to defy the regime. Perhaps they were simply good folk who created a life-saving network.

The network came to life at night when patrols—both Hlinka Guard and local informants—were less active. The peasants, villagers, traders, smugglers and go-betweens who created a web that encased the hamlets surrounding the estate made it their mission to get us out and give us a chance at life. Whoever those people were, whatever became of them, I am grateful to them, for I owe them everything.

I wonder what went through Giska's mind when, in the middle of the night, she was forced to hand her nephew and niece, two small children, to paid guides who would take them on the first leg of their perilous journey. My mind was blank when they wrapped us in blankets and placed us in a horse-drawn wagon under cover of darkness. The numbing terror that had hit me in the train station in Žilina was back with a vengeance. Bella remained hiding in Nitra until after Bubi and I left. Then Giska sent her to my grandparents in Vác, Hungary. Turi was sent to the Rombach Synagogue in Budapest, which had become a camp for refugee children.

Our safe haven had dissolved into mist.

Recalling the event years later, Bubi told me we left Aunt Giska's estate on an icy night in late

November. Barely awake, we were bundled into a horse-drawn cart, driven by a peasant who posed as our father. To the casual observer, we looked like a classic peasant

Near the Hungarian border.

family, slowly heading home to our little farmhouse just down the road. But the farmhouse we were headed for belonged to a nameless peasant in a nameless village about 15 miles from the legendary Blue Danube River and the Hungarian border, just that much closer to our goal of Budapest.

I must have been fast asleep as our "hosts" hustled us into the hayloft above the kitchen. They told Bubi not to move around and to make sure that when we woke up, we stayed absolutely silent.

When I opened my eyes a few short hours later, I found that without moving my head, I could see the countryside from the round window of the loft. The farmhouse was on a hill—I know because there were wide, snow-covered meadows as far as the eye could see. They were a beautiful trap. Anyone who walked across those fields would leave footprints and that made me afraid. Bubi was still sleeping, and I gripped his hand tightly, unable and unwilling to let go. The scene at the Žilina train depot was burned into my memory; my insecurity had not lessened one iota, and the screaming for my Papa and Mama was still going on in my head.

The fresh hay I was laying on tickled my nose. It was warm, soft and so deep I couldn't feel the floor beneath me. As the sun came over the horizon, the snow turned pink, but soon the clouds took over and the day, like our lives, turned a dismal gray.

We were in dangerous territory. With the Hungarian border so close, Jew-hunting raids came swiftly and often — they knew Jews were looking for ways to get into Hungary and that local peasants often hid them. Those who were helping us could never be too careful, for everyone's lives were at stake.

I soon became aware of adult voices drifting up from below through the slats of the hayloft floor, and understood what they were saying. They were talking about how they would smuggle Bubi and me into Budapest.

"Late tonight," said a female voice. "I will set out with the boy for Budapest. The little girl will stay. She is too skinny for such a long walk; it's too much for such a tiny child. She will hold us back and there will be trouble. Tonight, just the boy will cross the border. We will keep the little girl with us, here. She could be helpful and a delight; and it will be nice to have a child around."

From the depths of my being, an inner scream wanted to break loose with a shrieking, giant "NO!" But I stayed silent. That resolute will to survive was back. My feeling was that God, and now my Papa,

The young Judith.

were watching over me and commanding me to live. This emotion was stronger than ever as I remembered Papa's last words to me, yelled with an urgency I never forgot: "Go and live!"

I dared not close my eyes and fall asleep. I dreaded the possibility that they would steal Bubi away from me in the dark of night, and I would be left alone with these strangers forever.

When the peasants came to get Bubi—and only Bubi—that power and determination to live began to pump through my soul. I gripped Bubi's hand and at the top of my lungs, I shouted "NO!" at my rescuers. "NO! and NO! I am not staying. I don't want to be here." I screamed. I wept. I could not be silenced. I repeated my tearful mantra: "No, no, and no!" "No" was the only word I could articulate.

No safeguards. No parents. No stability. No secure family—and no more separation! Through the agony of irrevocable losses, knowing the world was a dangerous place, I understood that Bubi was my only lifeline, the most important connection to my roots, to my past. He confirmed my own sense of identity; I would not be parted from him. I would not relinquish my last link to my nuclear family. And so I would not let go of Bubi's hand. If I stayed fastened to him, they could not part us—nothing could part us.

Perhaps they understood me; perhaps they decided that keeping me against my will would be more dangerous or cruel than letting me go. One thing is certain: They could have kept me in that house if they wanted to. My scrawny fingers were no match for an adult's strength. Those grownups in charge of my fate could have forced me to stay behind, and who knows what route my life would have taken then? But they didn't do that. They let me go with Bubi.

That same night, Bubi and I, disguised as the children of the peasant woman who had prompted my hysteria, began the last leg of our journey. We wore peasant clothes and were instructed not to speak. We were to keep our eyes down and not draw attention to ourselves. It was made clear to us that this was not a game; it was a life-and-death situation. We needed no such reminders. Young as we were, Bubi and I understood the fragility of life.

The three of us set out just before midnight, heading southeast toward the Danube and the border. At first I walked strongly, without complaint. I wanted to prove I could do it. I wanted to show how brave I was. I was terrified they would send me back if I faltered, so I pushed myself. Through the snow and the freezing chill, I just kept going and going and going. In fact, I pushed too hard, and soon felt too weak to go on.

The peasant woman was right: I couldn't walk the whole way—the snow was nearly four feet deep and I was not much taller than the drifts. She stooped down and wordlessly hoisted me onto her back, as if I weighed next to nothing, and wrapped my arms around her neck. She held Bubi's hand in one hand and her peasant's sack in the other as we trudged through the night. My head, wrapped in a knitted peasant cap, rested on her shoulder.

We finally came to a main road where the walking would be easier. But suddenly the glaring headlights of a motorcycle blinded us. A policeman jumped off the vehicle and approached us. "Papers!" he demanded. I could feel the peasant woman's body go rigid, could sense her heartbeat quickening. In my fear, I snuggled closer, held her tighter, and pretended to be asleep.

"Where are you going?" He barked. "What are you doing on the road at this hour?"

Peasants were known to travel in the early hours of morning, so his question puzzled the woman. Without betraying her misgivings, she stood up to him.

"We are on our way to the next village, to visit my family," she said. The officer searched her sack, but found only bread, sausage and a jar of water. Satisfied that we weren't smuggling gold, diamonds or money, he grunted, and handed back the very valuable false papers he had taken from her.

Pushing ahead, we developed a slow rhythm as we plodded along the back roads in the snapping cold and deep darkness. As we drew nearer to the border and closer to first light, we were stopped a few more times by local police and Hlinka Guard patrols. Each time was more frightening than the last. And each time, the peasant woman convinced our tormentors that we were simply local travelers—unimportant, obscure, and exhausted, heading home in the night.

The country lanes nearer the border were well-traveled, and with growing numbers of people materializing around us, the danger of being caught increased exponentially. But there were benefits: The roads were easier to walk on, for the snow was firmly packed, and vehicular traffic had created low walls of snow and gravel on the shoulders, walls that would cover you if you needed to hide.

Suddenly we heard dogs barking viciously. They were the snarling dog packs the police and army used to track and trap refugees. The woman hustled us off the road, and threw me into a ditch behind the wall of snow and gravel. She crouched over us, her hands covering our mouths.

"Quiet!" she commanded.

At that moment, I imagined my eyes were as big as saucers in my ghostly white face. I shivered with panic and cold. I realized that in the short years of my existence, I had never lived in a world that was safe. It was all an illusion, a fact kept from me by loving parents and my childish innocence. But as I lay in that icy ditch, I instinctively knew that we were facing a point of no return. Huddled behind that snow and gravel wall, with the peasant woman's body over mine, I understood I had to be brave. Inside, I cried for Mama to come and protect me or take me away from the danger. But that would never happen, and I knew it. Once again, I could feel God and Papa watching, and they were giving me the wherewithal to endure.

I stayed quiet. I stayed brave. As the sky began to lighten almost imperceptibly, I peeked over the lip of the ditch. My eyes saw many boots — the shiny black boots of the border guards. Against the gray landscape, those brilliantly polished black boots seemed to shine and loom threateningly above me like the freshly painted bars of a prison cell.

The three of us stayed unmoving in that ditch for what seemed like eternity. It was fully dawn before there was a sudden commotion made by men, dogs, and vehicles — and then it was quiet at last. The border patrol had moved on. The peasant woman stood up slowly, surveyed the scene, and yanked us onto the road. At that moment, I yearned for my mother's embrace, for an approving hug for having done exactly as I was told. Instead, I received the abrupt, almost claw-like plucking of a stranger.

Stiff and cold, we ran along the road to a small bridge that led to safe haven. The woman presented our false papers to the lone border guard. We tramped across that bridge over the Danube into Hungary and kept on going until we came to a small farmhouse in a village just inside the border, the last way station on our route.

Bubi and I were taken up a wooden staircase to a small room and put to bed. We fell asleep holding hands. After what seemed like only a few moments, I opened my eyes to find someone holding me and putting a finger against my lips, warning me to be quiet. Then I was shoved unceremoniously under the bed and Bubi was thrust in beside me. Featherbeds, blankets, and pillows were stuffed around us like baby bumpers. Then the door to the room was closed and it was dark once more.

We immediately understood what had happened. Someone had seen us coming into the village and reported the presence of strange children to the authorities. Ever on the alert for a stray Jew, the local gendarmes arrived at the farmhouse and banged on the door. I could hear the familiar sound of stomping boots, reminding me of our terrible last day together as a family in Žilina, and I can only imagine the discussion that took place between our hunters and the peasant couple below.

"Children?"

"There are no children here!" the peasant responded. "A beggar woman came by earlier carrying a sack, but there were no children with her. This house wouldn't be so quiet if there were children here, now would it?"

"Can we search?"

"You need to search? Certainly, but first, have some beer. After all, you've been working so hard…"

Bubi and I huddled together under the bed, trying to disappear into the bedding that surrounded us. The voices below grew calmer, easier. Soon there was laughter. There was no search. The gendarmes never came upstairs.

I may have fallen asleep after that. Perhaps I dreamed again of Mama, of Papa, of a safe home. It was a comforting dream that came often—but it was just a dream.

The next day we were brought to a train station in a small town and another peasant woman took us to Budapest, less than 30 miles away. The city was amazing and huge, the biggest, most bustling place I had ever seen in my young life. The streets were wide boulevards lined with immense and beautiful buildings, but the snow was black with grime—slushy and dirty. I later learned that Budapest was called the Paris of Eastern Europe, but my child's mind couldn't grasp what that meant. The thousands of people swarming around us were busy and in a hurry; and amidst the chaos, the peasant woman managed to wend her way to the home of our maternal aunt, Margit Katz.

Exhausted, dirty and frightened, we were like pilgrims arriving at a shrine. Here at last, having survived so many dangers, was our refuge, our haven, and our family, though if I'd met Margit Katz before that day I am too young to remember it. As a family in hiding, always on the move, our lack of connection to our extended family was hardly surprising. True, my aunt was a stranger to me, but she was my mother's eldest sister—the oldest of five children. Margit was blood of my blood, flesh of my flesh. We two small children, lost, orphaned and alone in the world, had risked everything to land on her doorstep.

Our arrival must have been an enormous shock. In retrospect, I realize Giska must have had no way of letting Margit know that she was sending us to Budapest to be cared for. It was clear Aunt Margit was stunned to see three strangers, two of them young children, standing on her stoop when she opened her door to our guide's knock.

No one had spoken of the risks this would pose to Margit's own family. Her fears were very real; for, while Miklós Horthy de Nagybánya, the Regent of the Kingdom of Hungary, may have been protective of Hungary's Jews, it was nevertheless against the law to harbor those who were fleeing the Nazis or the Hlinka Guard. Any violation of this law — aiding refugees in any way — was punishable by death.

Aunt Margit cried. Remorseful, torn between fear and guilt, she begged the peasant woman to find another way to save us, and then told us we had to go. We were turned away. My aunt had her own family to think of. To add two small children who did not speak Hungarian to her brood of four was life-threatening. How long would it be before the neighbors noticed us? How long would it take for someone, or one of us, to give ourselves away?

Bubi and I stood shivering on our aunt's doorstep, two tiny but very real threats to Margit's family. She wept as she sent us away — her sister's children — so small and tired and solemn. She wept as she explained the facts of life to the peasant woman and pleaded with her to take care of us. "They will be safer with you," she told the woman. And then she turned her face away and shut the door.

It is impossibly painful to consider the agony of Margit's choiceless choice on that freezing November day in 1942. The rejection of two innocent children went deep. But I cannot condemn her, though she might have been consigning us to deportation and death. At best, she had delivered us to the vagaries of fortune when fortune did not smile on Jewish children.

Margit and three of her children survived the war. So did we. Who, in her place, would have acted otherwise? I have no idea what my own choices would have been under such circumstances, so I will not attempt to second-guess her.

Our peasant guide was taken aback. She had no intention of caring for us or bringing us back to the village people who had hidden us. She did what she thought was right. She took us to a park in Budapest, near a police station, sat us down on a public bench and told us to stay there. Then she left. She had done her job, discharged her responsibility. It was no fault of hers that her special delivery was rejected. Mission accomplished, she boarded a train back to her village while Bubi and I sat on the bench, holding onto each other, waiting to see what would happen next.

People passed us by as busy city-dwellers do, assuming, if they thought about us at all, that we were waiting for our parents. We were two children, alone with their false

Winter in a Budapest park.

papers, with nowhere to go and nothing to eat. We had no idea what would happen if it started to rain or snow or if the temperature would drop, so we stayed put. I silently prayed for God and Papa to watch over us.

Eventually, a policeman came over. He spoke to us in Hungarian. We answered in Czech, and were whisked away to the Conti Street Prison—a blessing disguised as Hell. At least we would have a roof over our heads to protect us from the winter weather and we would have some sort of food to eat. As for the rest... who knew what would happen? One could only hope for some respite.

The Conti Street prison in Budapest was irrevocably linked to violence and human suffering. It was smack in the middle of Budapest's notorious red light district and its inmates included common criminals and the wretched human refuse that any society generates, especially in the midst of war. It was also the pre-war home of the Hungarian Army's counter-intelligence department and was later used by the Arrow Cross, the Hungarian fascists and Nazi allies, to hold political dissidents.

Bubi and I were simply detritus, dregs of the Jewish people—a source of amusement to some of our captors and a moral puzzle to others. Once we had been wanted by the Slovak regime, now we were wanted by nobody. Our heads were shaved—standard operating procedure for all prisoners—and we were placed alone in a cell with a caged gate. Unlike the criminals and political dissents, we were not issued uniforms; we had only the clothes on our backs. From our cell, we could see rows of other steel cages — we were the only children in that place at that time, and we were granted no special mercies.

What I remember most was the horrible smell. It was a deadly mix of corrupt odors — disease, decay, decomposition, filth, sweat, vermin, excrement, and death. It was sour, foul, gross and heightened our sense of approaching terror. Equally frightening was the way people grabbed at me when Bubi and I were brought to the courtyard each day for some air and a bit of exercise.

As a pretty child with big, bright green eyes — "magnetic eyes," Mama used to call them — neighbors would invariably pat my head or hold me while they chatted with her on their way home from the market or other errand. I was used to being an object of attraction to adults, but not the kind of menacing, perverted, salacious attraction aimed at me in that repulsive hell hole. Some of them, in fact, were decent and tried to be kind and protective. But the ones who scared me most were the ones who seemed no longer human.

They grabbed at my shaved scalp and at my limbs, snatched at my coat, my shoes, and the wool stockings that covered my skinny legs. They crowded around me and Bubi. They loomed over us, snarling like pack animals about to spring on their prey, seemingly reduced to creatures who sniffed and poked at fresh meat before they ripped it to shreds.

Even when we were "safe" in our cell, the sounds they made were shocking and penetrated to the deepest parts of our brains. By day there were screams, shouts and shrieking obscenities; at night there were wails and moans and weeping—the sorry sounds human misery and pain produce. It was certainly not the best early-childhood education program for two impressionable youngsters.

The memories of that place make me shudder to this day. That awful place was home to us for weeks. We shared it with the rats that scurried over our ankles as we slept, and with the fleas and lice that took up residence in the folds of our skin and laid their eggs in the fresh bristle growing on our heads. Once a week the guards scraped a thick, small-toothed comb over our heads to catch the lice lurking in the stubble, and then poured petroleum over us. They were not gentle about it and hurt us when they could get away with it. On those days, the prison stench was worse than usual, as the noxious smell mingled with the already dreadful miasma around us. We were almost always sick to our stomachs.

We had no idea if anyone even knew we existed. For all we knew we might soon find ourselves on a train very much like the one that took Robi and Rena, Mama and Papa away from us. We didn't speak to each other much, Bubi and I. What was there for us to say? I know he tried to protect me as best he could. He was sweet and caring, but there was nothing he could do. Still, I never let go of him. Never. I slept holding onto his clothing so that if he moved in the night, it would wake me. I ate sitting close beside him. When he went to the toilet, I was there. I would not let him out of my sight. Not for a minute.

What does it take to keep a child alive? Food, water, shelter. That's all you need. Nourishment of the spirit, the soul, and the emotions requires love. What happens to a child when love is abruptly taken away and replaced by constant, insistent terror?

I would find out.

Bubi and I languished in our prison cell for at least two weeks, filthy, scared, and utterly alone. It must have been the end of November when we first arrived. We had no clue that the Jewish Rescue Committee in Budapest was busy trying to get us out of prison, no idea that they were aware of our existence. There was no way for us to know that the Budapest Jewish community was stirred to action on our behalf. I am guessing that my family in Budapest contacted the Jewish underground, but I will never be sure.

We found out later that word had leaked from the prison. A rumor about two Czech-speaking children, presumably Jewish, was spreading through the city and found its way to the underground network. Hungary was not yet occupied by Germany, so the Hungarian Jews put what little autonomy they had to good use. Later I learned they were also connected to Rabbi Weissmandl's Working Committee.

Ironically, on Chanukah, the Jewish festival of lights that commemorated miracles during Temple times in ancient Israel, Bubi and I would soon see the light at the end of our own dark tunnel. Unbeknownst to Bubi and me, a kindly watchmaker by the name of Teitelbaum/Tenenbaum (I am unsure of his name) had heard about us and decided to do something about our situation.

Teitelbaum/Tenenbaum was eager to get us out of the prison as fast as he could — if only to get us some respite from the relentlessness of our situation. We don't know how it happened, but on the last night of Chanukah, December 10, 1942, Bubi and I were suddenly removed from our bleak prison cage and whisked to a comfortable, middle-class Jewish home in the heart of the Jewish quarter of Budapest. It was indeed a Chanukah miracle.

To this day, I do not know how Teitelbaum/ Tenenbaum got us out, and I have since tried to find his family with no success. He took us from the Conti Street prison to an apartment not far away. When he opened the door, our astonished eyes saw the golden flames of eight candles emanating from a gleaming silver menorah dancing before our eyes. It brought me back at once to our family's special Sabbath celebrations in Piešťany — eight candles, one for each family member, Mama's sparkling candlesticks, the white tablecloth, the feeling of being protected by our family's love and God's love. There they all were, in the watchmaker's household — all the things I recognized and yearned for: family, faith, ritual, security. I had almost forgotten such things existed, and this rediscovery was jarring.

How kind they were! They bathed us and gave us a new change of clothing; they showered us with cookies and candies, fed us well, and they didn't forget the potato pancakes. We even played dreidel — spinning the top with the letters that stood for the Hebrew words: "A great miracle occurred there."

I wanted to bask forever in the homey warmth of the Teitelbaum/Tenenbaum's apartment, where so much resembled what we had lost. It was like Cinderella's fairy tale. I was certain that when the clock chimed a certain hour, this respite, this luxury, this love would disappear and Bubi and I would wake up in our cell, in rags, filthy and frightened.

I had no glass slipper to leave behind. How would anyone who cared ever find me again? I didn't want to ask for the things I wanted, but I wanted more. I had thick stockings and torn gloves when I arrived at the prison, now I was wearing serviceable clothing. I was well-fed. I was almost happy.

My feeling that the dream could not last was correct. Teitelbaum/Tenenbaum had only been able to secure a limited reprieve. When the clock struck the hour, he took us back to Conti Street and made a solemn vow before he left: "I promise you won't stay here long. I will make sure we get you out. I will find somebody to take care of you. Just behave yourselves—be very, very good children—and be patient. Somebody will come for you. I promise."

Teitelbaum/Tenenbaum's gift of hope was the best Chanukah gift I could have imagined. It made it a little easier to go back to the fearsome wildness of the prison. In the few hours we were gone, nothing had changed in that hellish place and the nightmare was upon us once more—made sharper by the interlude of peace in the Teitelbaum/Tenenbaum's apartment. We had no idea how long it would be before his promise to us would be fulfilled, but at last we had hope.

In an extraordinary coincidence, Teitelbaum/ Tenenbaum saw Maurice and Ilonka Stern, a childless couple who owned the most famous kosher restaurant in Budapest, and told them about us. Could the Sterns free us from the Conti Street prison? They could and they did, and — miraculously — Bubi and I were soon under their protection.

CHAPTER FIVE
The Sterns

The amazing Sterns were able to do many wonderful things for people in the Jewish community because of their famous restaurant. Located in the center of the Jewish Quarter, diagonally across the street from the famous Rumbach Synagogue, it had a reputation for marvelous food and excellent service—a reputation that attracted patrons from near and far and from all walks of life. Everyone was treated like royalty. It was even rumored that Vice-Admiral Horthy, the head of the Hungarian government, and his son enjoyed meals there on a regular basis, especially the *cholent*. Refugees from all over Europe would come in for coffee or tea and socialize, planning and scheming, hoping to find a way to escape.

Everyone loved the Sterns and considered them elite members of the Jewish social circles in Budapest. Maurice Stern was discreet, he was respectful, and he knew his place. He was Marci to his wife and friends, often called Stern *Bácsi* (pronounced *batchi*—meaning

Maurice and Ilonka Stern, proprietors of
Stern's Kosher Restaurant on Rombach Street.

uncle), a respectful Hungarian honorific, by almost
everyone else. I called him *Apu* (Hungarian for Papa).

He was a tall, elegant, imposing man with the
bespectacled look of a scholar. He was always
immaculately dressed, with the fob of his gold watch
slung just so across his vest front. When he went
outdoors, for any reason, he wore an impressive
Homburg and carried a carved walking stick. He had
big features: thick eyebrows over jet-black eyes, wide
ears, a prominent nose, and a square white beard.
Apu's courtliness and bonhomie were also the signature
characteristics of his restaurant, characteristics that had
contributed significantly to its success.

The goodwill that characterized his relationships
with the power elite provided the Sterns with a

layer of protection, especially since he was involved in underground rescue efforts. And since a busy restaurant always needs extra help — wait staff, dishwashers and bus boys — Stern was able to save people, including children, within the letter and spirit of the law by "hiring workers" for his business. We Mannheimers were hardly the first refugees to benefit from the Sterns' largesse. Over the years, the couple had also taken in relatives from other parts of Europe.

Stern's nephew, Matti Schwartz, his wife Baba, and son Riki, lived in the same building as the restaurant. They also worked there. The Sterns lived in a large apartment right next door, and Ilonka Stern's niece, Frieda Goldberger, her husband, and their young daughter, Judit, lived in the building, as well. The Goldbergers also worked in the restaurant. The Sterns knew they could keep us safe. Soon after we got there, they were even able to bring Turi and Bella to their home. I have no idea how it was all managed. All I know is that one evening our cell door was opened and that someone took us by the hand and led us away from that horrible, horrible prison. We were told we were going to the east side of the Danube River, to a house on Rumbach Street, in the epicenter of the Jewish quarter in Pest. The Dohany Synagogue, the most elegant in all of Hungary, was within walking distance. We heard what we were being told, but we barely understood it and found what we did understand hard to believe. It was all so remarkable to us.

We walked out of that stinking prison leaving the wreckage of humanity behind. We were shown to a

On a visit to Hungary many years later,
the Stern's residence front entrance.

The courtyard and restaurant's back door.

horse-drawn carriage waiting at the curb, climbed in and were driven through the streets of the city, rocking gently and being soothed by the sound of the horseshoes clip-clopping on the cobblestones. I sat staring out the window, transfixed by the sights and lights. A good while later, the carriage stopped in front of a large apartment house, number 10 Rumbach Street.

Someone tried to help me step out of the carriage, but, as usual, I wouldn't let go of Bubi's hand. I was bewildered when we walked through a porte-cochére into a cobblestoned courtyard. I looked up in the dark to see that we were surrounded on four sides by a massive brick building with wrought-iron balconies running the length of each floor. Dimly lit windows ran in straight, draped rows behind the railings. We had no idea where we were or what would happen next.

Ilonka Stern — whom people called *Néni* (pronounced *naynee*), meaning aunt — was waiting for us. I soon called her *Anyu* (Mommy). We didn't know who she was or that we were looking at the woman who would take care for us from that moment on. She was fair and tall, with an ample build and the face of an angel. Her delicate features, a narrow nose and aristocratic mouth, were evenly centered on a round face. Her sweet personality shone through her eyes, attracted people to her and held them close. She

Ilonka Stern.

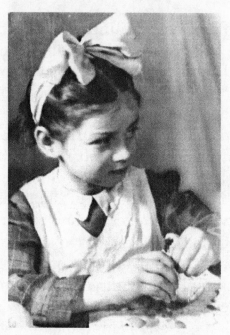
My first photo taken in Budapest.

stood in front of us and with a kind look led us into the restaurant on the ground floor.

To my young eyes it seemed a vast place, opulently appointed with its elegant white tablecloths, regal high-backed chairs, and a regiment of uniformed staff waiting to serve.

Then she took me by the hand and led me upstairs to the family apartment on the third floor. The apartment was huge, with lots of windows. Glass pocket doors separated the rooms and were lined in lace. The kitchen was darker and separated the master suite from the other rooms—many bedrooms, parlors, and staff quarters. It was the most beautiful apartment I had ever seen.

I understood, standing there in awe, that Tenenbaum/Teitelbaum's promise to find us a safe and comfortable home was fulfilled—a promise kept. But I no longer felt I belonged in such a place, as much as I wanted to be part of it. I was grimy and grubby, a prison rat in disheveled clothes. My face was gaunt and dirty. I still wore the little hand-knitted peasant cap I had worn on that snowy night on the last leg of our journey to Hungary. It covered what was once my silken hair and was now just stubble. After all my deprivation and all the horror, I felt lost when confronted with such luxury and began to cry. I wanted to live there and didn't believe it was real.

Ilonka *Néni* gently drew me into the kitchen, sat down at the table, undid my cap and folded me into her arms. I could feel her warmth seeping into me, and I knew I never wanted her to let me go. I wanted to stay in her arms forever and never be cold again. Quietly she held me until she felt my body lose its tension and relax in her embrace. I melted, never wanting to let go or move away, afraid that if I did, I would lose her forever, that the dream would evaporate as it had so many times before. That moment in her arms marked the end of my privation.

From that instant on, I was given everything I had been lacking for so long: safety, food, shelter, cleanliness, and most importantly, the unconditional love I craved. At that moment they became my *Anyu* and *Apu*—my mother and father.

By the time I met them, the Sterns were middle-aged — old enough to be my grandparents — and seemed to carry themselves with an air of magisterial authority. Yet there was nothing aloof about them. They became true parents to me during the few years I spent with them, and they showered me with love. They are the parents I remember more vividly than I do my own beloved and lost Mama and Papa.

I really know very little about them, for although

The Sterns on a forest hike.

they lived the majority of their lives before they came into mine, I was too young to be curious about them and did not ask. They did not volunteer, and I was, after all, a child focused solely on their impact on my life.

They were delightful, with lively personalities and good humor that lived side-by-side with their dignity. They took joy in hiking through the forest, dressed in their best. *Anyu* might sit on a rock to rest, wearing a fashionable cloche and a fur stole carelessly slung across her shoulders. *Apu* would stand near her in his bespoke suit, wearing his Homburg and leaning on his walking stick — so debonair.

But great tragedy was no stranger in their lives. Years earlier they had lost their only child, a son, to disease. The Sterns' grief was deeply held and rarely expressed. I never knew their son's name, never learned exactly when he had died or from what, but the tragedy had left a hole in the Sterns' lives that could never be filled, they said, until I came along. For while *Apu* and *Anyu* took in all my siblings and saved our lives, while they fed, clothed, educated and cared for us all, they loved me almost to distraction. I became the child who filled the void.

I suppose it was because I was the baby — they told me I was cute — with big, green, questioning eyes and a vulnerable manner. They took great pleasure in giving me whatever I asked for, instantly fulfilling my wishes. But there was more to it than that. I wasn't simply a precious doll to dress and feed and spoil. The Sterns understood, far better than I, what the terrors of the last few months had done to me. They understood how years of hiding and fear had affected me. They were fully aware of the losses I and the others had suffered. They seemed to know what such misery could do to so young a child. They sensed intuitively, without my saying a word, that I could not bear to be left alone, and they made sure it never happened.

Anyu assigned a nanny who was ordered never to leave my side. I slept in the Sterns' bedroom, in a bed at the foot of theirs, so if a nightmare woke me in the middle of the night they would be right there. They hugged me continually and for as long as I needed to be held; they seemed to understand how hungry I was for demonstrations of affection, and they never withheld love from me — not ever. To this day I can still feel the power of *Anyu*'s embrace, warm and soft, her arms encircling me as I snuggled in, happy to be there. I can still feel how reassuring it was when *Apu* would take my little hand in his great big hand, so strong and steady.

Their love was my security, so that steadily and surely, in time, I was weaned away from Bubi and didn't need to clutch his hand or keep him in my sight at every moment. In time, as the love kept coming, and I learned that I would not be abandoned, I once again began to feel safe. And, in return, I hope I was able to make up a little bit for their lost son by returning their deep love and giving them the respect and honor they so richly deserved.

Turi had managed to get to Budapest and was in the refugee camp for children right there on Rumbach Street, in the now "former" synagogue. From there, orphaned and abandoned children were usually sent back to their countries of origin. Turi was in danger of being deported to Slovakia, but happily, an official at the camp took a liking to him and decided to help.

The official, like Vice-Admiral Horthy, frequented Stern's

The Rombach Street Synagogue.

famous restaurant. He was friendly with the Sterns, who were stalwarts of the city's Jewish community. When he told the Sterns that there was an abandoned Jewish boy from Slovakia at the refugee camp, the Sterns immediately asked that Turi be freed and brought to live with them.

Bella, as well, had made it to Budapest. Originally Giska had intended to send her to Vác, but instead she wound up in a camp for refugee children near a Jewish hospital. She too, wound up in the Stern household.

My special relationship with the Sterns did not go unnoticed by my siblings or the other children in the household — Riki and Judit. There was no hiding it, and the Sterns did not try to. Not surprisingly, the others were jealous, most especially my sister Bella. Understandably,

Reunited Mannheimer siblings in Budapest with Riki, a new friend.

Bella resented the fact that I was treated like a princess who never had to lift a finger, while she was expected to help out in the restaurant and do chores. It created a distance between us.

One day, Bella, who was sweeping the floor, asked me to grab the dustpan and help her.

"No," I said petulantly. "I don't have to."

It made Bella so angry she swiped me with the broom. "Yes, you do," she insisted. But it wasn't true, and we both knew it. I really didn't have to do anything. I could simply run to *Anyu* and *Apu* and ask for a hug and wrap either or both of them around my little finger.

I learned something from this. I learned that being a cute child and acting vulnerable—"needy" would not be too strong a word—brought me the affection I sought. And with affection came security. A lifetime later, I now understand that this need to win people over was a survival tactic, one I would draw on often in my young years.

The Sterns' love gave me the strength I would need in the years that followed. Their love carried healing power; it allowed me to let go of my past and, in their presence, begin putting together the foundation that would allow me to construct a new life. The terror and loss of the past were slowly and surely scraped away by their affection and care. No two people could have given me more, and I shudder to think what my life would have been like if the Sterns had not become my *Anyu* and *Apu* from January 1943 to sometime in 1946.

Though Europe was collapsing, for us children the years we spent with the Sterns were wonderful, truly golden years. While Bella, Bubi and Turi each attended their own schools, for the first time in my life, I went to a real school myself—the Jewish school on Dob Street, where I was assigned to the first grade. My nanny walked me there each day, although it wasn't far, just down the block and around the corner. At first, my inability to speak Hungarian isolated me from the other children, and as a result, they resented me. This made me unhappy, of course, but the helpful attention of my teachers compensated somewhat for my loneliness.

School was a very formal place. Each student sat at her or his own desk with a straight back and slanted desktop that lifted into a drawer where school supplies were kept. We had to sit up straight, and when we weren't writing or holding a book, our hands had to be kept behind our backs. Of course, you had to raise your hand for permission to speak, to answer a question, or to ask if you could be excused to go to the toilet.

Everything we learned in those days was by rote, and while I didn't understand what the teacher was saying, I could easily copy whatever was written on the blackboard. When we were taught the ABCs, we were instructed to create designs out of the letters. In this exercise, my artistic talent came to the fore, and I was praised for my drawings. Such approval helped me regain some confidence, too.

I was still very shy and didn't like to raise my hand for any reason. One day, I really needed to relieve myself but I simply couldn't raise my hand to ask for permission to leave the room. It was too embarrassing. To add to my stress, I still harbored "bathroom" fears from that miserable episode in the outhouse, and I was afraid to bring attention to myself. So I held it in—and fainted.

Needless to say, such behavior did not earn me the respect of my peers, and though I soon was able to speak and understand Hungarian, I lacked the linguistic ease of those children for whom it was a mother tongue. During recess, when the girls gathered to jump rope, I was invariably shunted aside. I would indicate with signs and gestures that I was willing to turn the rope, but nobody paid any attention to me.

One day, when the girls were clearly looking for someone to turn the rope, I managed to overcome my shyness long enough to step forward and hold out my hand. Vera Czik, the school beauty and the most popular girl in the class, took one look at my outstretched hand, slapped my face and pushed me away. I fell and began to cry. A teacher picked me up and took me to the principal's office. The principal called the Sterns, who came and brought me home.

This incident of schoolyard bullying became something of a crisis. The Sterns were not satisfied to bring me home, comfort me, and forget the hurt that had been done. They wanted to protect their precious child. If the school couldn't guarantee my acceptance by the other children, they could at least ensure my safety. The Sterns met with the principal to demand that bullying behavior be stopped and punished.

The principal called Vera's parents in to discuss the issue. Both sets of parents sat in the school office with the principal between them.

"No child should be treated this way, especially this child," *Apu* announced. He explained that I was an orphan from Sovakia who, screaming, had seen her parents shoved into a cattle car with her siblings, never to see them again. He told them how Bubi and I, disguised as peasant children, had crossed the border into Hungary, where we had been rejected by our own family members and were abandoned in the streets as if we were dogs. He told them how Bubi and I were "arrested" and held in the Conti Street prison for weeks, and how he'd learned about us from the watchmaker.

In the course of the telling, Stern noticed that Vera's father had grown pale, that he was listening with rapt attention. Finally, he spoke and asked Stern pointed questions about me: What was my family name? Who was my father? What were the names of my Hungarian grandparents, and where had they lived? He wanted to know detail after detail.

Finally, the mystery unraveled. Czik suspected, from the tale Stern was telling, that he and my mother were cousins, and Stern's answers confirmed the fact. Only now was he learning of her deportation and death, only now did he realize that the child his daughter had slapped and pushed was his own kin.

He was in shock. Tears rolled down his face as his heart opened to me. It changed everything. Now Vera and I were family, and she and her parents couldn't do enough for me. Vera became my mentor, my guardian and my best friend. That, of course, was like a magic door opening, and gave me instant acceptance at school.

From then on, everything Vera's parents did for her they also did for me. When Vera got a new outfit, so did

I. I have an old photo that shows me decked out in one of those ensembles, a soft woolen suit with the military look that was the latest fashion trend: a long tunic, with gold braid on the sleeves, and a cap set rakishly on my head. The stubble of my prison days had by then grown into long braids, tied with big, bright ribbons. There are rings on my fingers, a shoulder bag over my left arm, and a glowing smile on my face.

The smile was real. For me, life in Budapest at that time was truly a paradise. I lived in great comfort and luxury. I was part of an extended family that included my surviving siblings, the Schwartzes, the Goldbergers, the Cziks and Riki's cousin, Yossi.

I had many friends and playmates in the building, many of them non-Jews. We all played together without ever having to leave the building, racing back and forth along the balcony that overlooked the courtyard. It was a blissful, happy time.

Once a week I went to ballet lessons, which awakened a passion that has lasted all my life. In the summertime we crossed the bridges from Pest to Buda and went into the hills to stay at a country resort for a few weeks. If we stayed in the city, we would take the ferry to Margit Island perched in the Danube, where we would picnic, swim in the huge pool and frolic in the playground.

We also visited my maternal grandmother, Ethel Neumann Ungar, in Vác. I remembered how picking berries in the orchard behind her house gave me some comfort, and so the Sterns were able to provide me with warm memories of my maternal grandmother. (My grandfather died in 1940; my grandmother was deported in May 1944.)

With Riki and Yossi.

The Sterns even re-established our connection to Aunt Margit, who had closed the door in Bubi's face and mine just a year earlier. Sometimes, her children played with us in the park. On occasion, they would take me to the movies. Not a word was ever said, in my hearing, about my aunt's refusal to take us in. We concentrated on being a family.

A steady diet of good food and constant love made me strong and healthy, though I did suffer from normal childhood ailments. After I had my tonsils taken out in the doctor's office, I was plied with ice cream and gifts to compensate for the ordeal. And when I woke up one night with a terrible toothache, *Anyu* took me to her bed and held me until morning. If I caught cold, *Apu* would rock me on his lap and let me pull his beard until we both laughed. They spoiled me like grandparents, loved me as their own child, and I was overjoyed.

In Budapest's still thriving Jewish community, the poor were taken care of and could always find something to eat at the Sterns. *Shabbat* and the holidays were celebrated in the city without fear. At Passover, the Sterns traditionally set a table in the restaurant and invited at least fifty of the city's poorest and hungriest Jews. That was in keeping with the spirit of the holiday—"Let all who are hungry come and eat"—and with the charity the Sterns regularly practiced. Those huge Seders were wonderful occasions, but they went on for hours. I remember the Hungarian matzo balls, small and hard as golf balls, but I liked them that way, and ate a lot of them. Having a full belly, as well as the late hour, may well have contributed to my falling asleep at the table right after the entrée—and the Seder service would drone on around me, acting as a lullaby, well into the wee hours of the morning.

In the early days of 1944, the Hungarian Jewish community was blessed with a visit of momentous importance from the Belzer Rebbe, Rabbi Aharon Rokeach. A man of distinguished lineage, great learning, great fame and great spiritual significance, he was the grandson of Rabbi Shalom Rokeach, who founded the Belzer Hasidic movement in 1817 that by 1943 had tens of thousands of followers.

During the Rebbe's visit, the restaurant was closed to the public and converted into a rabbinical court, where the Rebbe gave audiences to thousands of petitioners who sought his advice or blessings. It seemed like the line of people waiting to see him was endless, stretching as it did down Rumbach Street and around the corner onto Dob Street.

One evening, the Rebbe joined the Stern family for *Shabbat* dinner, an unusually high honor. When the Belzer Rebbe made *Kiddush* over the wine, the goblet was passed to me and my siblings so that each of us could take a sip of the blessed liquid. I knew virtually nothing about the Belzer Rebbe, his Hasidim, his history or his importance as a scholar and spiritual leader, but I was completely caught up in the excitement. As I sipped the wine, I could feel the thrill and awe that seemed to affect everyone at the table.

Belzer Rebbe, z"l.

During that dinner the Belzer Rebbe told my brother Bubi to flee and go to what was then Mandate Palestine and would later become the State of Israel. Coming from such an important person, such advice was taken very seriously, and soon the Sterns began making arrangements to get him there.

As for me, I was content and comfortable in my happy home with my adoring *Anyu* and *Apu* and my siblings. Although I paid less and less attention to my brother and sister, I was glad they were near me. I was cheerful in school, was studying in Hungarian, and learned more with each passing day. There were friends, outings, parties, toys, beautiful clothes and shoes—all the things I loved. I was even vaguely aware that 1943 had begun with an important German military defeat: the loss at Stalingrad. Everything, it seemed, was on the upswing. Everywhere, the signs were positive.

To keep me amused, *Anyu* and *Apu* Stern bought me the most beautiful porcelain dolls. They had human hair in ringlets, eyes that opened and closed, and limbs that moved. They also came with lots of outfits and dresses, shoes, socks and ribbons, and I spent hours upon hours joyfully playing with them. If something happened and one of the dolls broke an arm or a leg, we would rush off to the doll hospital, where my tiny patients would be treated with great care and respect, and returned to me in "like-new" condition.

I celebrated my sixth birthday in the beginning of fall 1943, shamelessly spoiled by my *Anyu* and *Apu*. As 1944 began, life could not have been better. It had taken more than a year, but I had clearly emerged from the sorrows and darkness that had dimmed the glow of Mama's Sabbath candles. I was encased in the redemptive light of a Hungarian Chanukah that seemed to last all year. I was safe, and saw no reason why life couldn't continue in this wonderful way forever.

Then, suddenly, in March 1944, the Germans invaded Hungary, and my world was turned upside down—again.

CHAPTER SIX
The Glass House

The German occupation capsized life at Number 10 Rombach Street—violently and at one stroke. The troops entered Budapest on March 19; on March 20, our lives were at risk. That day set in motion one of the cruelest episodes in a human disaster of unequalled cruelty.

The story of Hungary's Jews has been told in all its numbing detail time and again. Facing almost certain defeat on the battlefield, Hitler and his minions raced against time to destroy the last vestige of European Jewry, the 700,000 Hungarian Jews and the tens of thousands Jewish refugees who found a measure of safety in Hungary.

When the Germans learned that Horthy had given tacit approval for Prime Minister Miklós Kállay to negotiate a separate peace with the Russians, the Wehrmacht arrived to crush the Hungarians and occupy the country. Kallay was replaced by Prime Minister Dome Sztojay, an antisemite more than willing to implement the Final Solution. He eagerly placed himself at the service of Adolf Eichmann and his henchmen, who had been dispatched to Budapest to make quick work of the Jews. The day the Germans marched into Budapest, Hungary's borders were closed. The only way a Jew could leave was to be shot, get beaten to death, go up in smoke, or die in a labor camp.

Eichmann focused first on the Jews in the provinces and concentrated them in cities to prepare for their deportation. With the assistance of Hungarian clerks, policemen, soldiers, and gendarmes, Eichmann commandeered 147 trains and sent virtually all the Jews living outside Budapest—almost half a million people—to Auschwitz or labor camps between May 15 and July 8. Deportation for the 200,000 Jews of Budapest was also being planned, but our lives had already changed drastically for the worse. As soon as they got there, the Germans appointed a Jewish Council, instituted the anti-Jewish laws that were in effect in Poland and other German-occupied countries, severely restricted Jewish life, and in what heralded the coming nightmare more than anything else, required Jews to wear yellow stars.

On what seemed to me a weekly basis, Nazi SS officers, supported by Hungarian gendarmes, would drive up to our apartment house and shout for everyone to go to the courtyard. Terrified, people would come running out of their apartments; the staff would file out of the restaurant, and the courtyard would quickly be filled with nervous people, shaking with fear. This was called a "roundup."

The gendarmes lined us up in rows of five and each of us, in turn, would shout out our names as the SS men checked off their lists. Non-Jews were permitted to leave and go on about their business, but we Jews stood there for hours while we were scrutinized, as the Nazis counted us again and again and made sure we were wearing our yellow stars. Inside the building, the gendarmes would sweep through each floor, banging on doors, searching the apartments to see if anyone was hiding. Then they would help themselves to whatever took their fancy.

Bubi, Turi, Judith and Bela wearing their yellow stars, March 1944.

At first the roundups terrified me. I stood mutely between *Anyu* and *Apu*, clutching both their hands, and *Apu* answered for me when it came time for me to say my name. The Sterns themselves must have been frightened, for the onslaught had been sudden and unexpected. They and the rest of the Jewish community were in something approaching a state of shock. There was no place to hide or run to, and the walls of our world pressed in closer and tighter with each day, just as they had during my early childhood in Pieštany and Žilina.

Curfews were imposed, and at first we could go out for just three hours a day. Soon that was increased to six hours a day. I was a child who did not fit the Nazi stereotype of a Jew, so it was assumed that I could move about freely in the streets without attracting attention. I became the family's link to the outside world. Though it was dangerous, I enjoyed being out and about. It was an adventure to walk around the city almost on my own, with just the maid at my side and do things grownups were increasingly afraid to do.

As Jewish life in Budapest grew more restricted, my freedom became something the family relied on. For example, when *Apu* became ill and was hospitalized that spring, *Anyu* was too frightened to leave the apartment. She would prepare kosher food for him every day and I would accompany the non-Jewish maid as she carried it in a covered basket to the hospital.

I loved feeling that I was doing something important, something no one else could do. Sometimes the police would stop us and ask where we were going, but they were friendly, and I don't remember feeling fear, so I answered truthfully that I was visiting someone in the hospital.

A few weeks later, Turi needed an emergency appendectomy and was ordered to stay in bed to complete his recovery. He was supposed to lay still—a difficult task for an 11-year old boy under any circumstances, but Turi's fresh wound was still painful and he could hardly move. On the day he came home from the hospital, there was a roundup, and all of us except Turi went down to the courtyard. As we ran down the stairs, we passed the Hungarian gendarmes and SS officers on their way upstairs to loot the apartments. When they found Turi, they pulled him out from under the covers, threw him to the floor, kicked him, and beat him—for the fun of it, I suppose, or perhaps because his presence surprised them...or perhaps for no reason at all.

When the roll call was finally over, we came upstairs to find Turi bleeding and in agony on the floor. *Anyu* and *Apu* held him, hugged him, lifted him tenderly back onto his bed and washed his wounds. A maid was dispatched at once to fetch the doctor, who dressed Turi's wounds and warned him not to leave his bed. There was nothing more we could do for him. There was no one to appeal to for justice. We were Jews at the mercy of a formidable force that seemed bent on destroying us at any cost.

When I saw what happened to Turi, I clung to *Anyu* and *Apu* because I was as shaken and frightened as I had been before I found safety in their home.

In June, Eichmann rounded up 25,000 suburban Jews from the outskirts of Budapest and sent them to Auschwitz. The Hungarian authorities ordered the Jews inside Budapest to move into 2,000 designated buildings scattered throughout the city by June 16. Ours was one of the designated houses, marked, as they all were, with Stars of David. Soon all of our building's apartments were overcrowded with families from other districts. The Nazis had succeeded in creating an open ghetto in the Jewish quarter.

Now the Jews of Budapest could easily be found. We could be rousted and deported, one house at a time. From countryside to suburb to city, the Nazi predator, with its mouth open and teeth bared, was coming ever closer, looking to devour us completely.

On July 7, Horthy, yielding to personal pleas from the Pope Pius XII, President Roosevelt, Winston Churchill and King Gustav of Sweden, called a halt to the deportations. For the moment at least, those of us in Budapest had been spared. Throughout that long, hot summer of 1944, the Jews of Budapest worried about their fate and wondered how long it would take for the Allies to reach them. They worked hard at finding some means of escape or refuge. In this latter endeavor, at last, they had some help from the outside.

Raoul Wallenberg, a businessman whose partner was a Hungarian Jew, was dispatched to Budapest to join Per Anger as representatives of the Swedish government and as delegates of the War Refugee Board in America. They created safe houses by declaring certain buildings to be Swedish protectorates that could not be "invaded" by the Nazis. Then they issued "passes" to the desperate Jews and smuggled them into the houses. By war's end, Wallenberg and Anger saved tens of thousands of Jewish lives. (Wallenberg was arrested by the Russians soon after they took over the city. What they did to him and how he died remains a deep and enduring mystery.)

Carl Lutz.

Less well known, but essential to my story, was Carl Lutz, a Swiss diplomat — the vice-consul in Budapest in 1942. He represented fourteen nations, including the United States and Britain, and his main task was to care for nationals of those countries who were stranded in Hungary. His responsibility for British interests also gave him jurisdiction over emigration to Palestine. In 1942 and 1943, before the Germans marched into Hungary, Lutz, working with the Jewish Agency for Palestine, managed to help thousands of Jewish children and young people

The Glass House in Budapest.

reach Mandate Palestine. But after March 19, 1944, such escape became impossible.

Once the deportations to Auschwitz began, Lutz focused on saving as many Jewish lives in Budapest as possible. Aided by a growing staff of Jewish helpers ranging from left-wing secular Zionists to the ultra-Orthodox, Lutz established a Department of Emigration of the Swiss Legation and issued *Schutzbriefen* or *Schutzpasses*, letters declaring their holders to be under Swiss protection. Lutz is credited with "inventing" these protective letters, which Wallenberg and others emulated to save Jews. Lutz negotiated with the Nazis and the Hungarian government and received

Members of the Arrow Cross.

permission to issue 8,000 *Schutzpasses*. One of his tricks was to define the 8,000 "units" as families, not individuals.

Lutz settled his army of helpers into a former glass factory at 29 Vadasz Street. The two-story, glass-fronted building was just a few blocks north of the Jewish section and was known as the Glass House (*Üvegház*). As soon as the Glass House came under Swiss protection, Jews went there to apply for Lutz's passes, which were being issued non-stop. No *Schutzpass* was ever assigned a number above 8,000. Each batch of 1,000 names was grouped into a Swiss

Collective Passport, and thus everyone named in that passport was formally under Swiss protection.

Though the wolf was at the door — the Allies having slashed their way through the Wehrmacht in Western Europe, and the Russians shattering what was left of it in Eastern Europe — the Nazis and their collaborators were relentless in their attempts to kill every Jew they could before the Third Reich would fall to its knees in April 1945. On October 15, 1944, just to get at the Hungarian Jews, they engineered a *coup d'état* (a government overthrow) arrested Horthy and installed the Fascist Arrow Cross Party, under Ferenc Szalási, as Hungary's leaders.

The very next day, Szalasi imposed a total curfew on Jews, essentially putting us all under house arrest for the next five days. On the sixth day, we could go out to take care of whatever business we had for two hours. But inside or out, we were no longer safe. Armed Arrow Cross thugs, called *Nyilas*, had carte blanche to conduct a reign of terror against us, and did so with relish. Jews were kidnapped from their homes; their homes were plundered. Hundreds of people were shot; their corpses piled high in a bloody display outside the Dohany Synagogue. Hundreds more were drafted for brutal forced labor, earning them a slower and more painful death.

Better to be shot!

On October 23, the government issued orders for Jewish men aged 16 to 60 and Jewish women aged 16 to 40 to report for slave labor. Luckily there was a loophole. Those with foreign passports or other legal documents placing them under the protection of other countries were exempt. Suddenly, even the skeptics understood the life-saving value of Lutz's *Schutzpasses*. The lines outside the Glass House grew into a crushing crowd.

Lutz and his staff worked prodigiously as the Allies drew closer and the Arrow Cross and Nazis grew more deadly. From November 1944 through January 1945, the Legation managed to issue thousands of *Schutzpasses*. Thousands more were issued by the International Committee of the Red Cross, headed by another Swiss national, Friedrich Born. And young Jewish activists made the Glass House their base of operations for daring rescues of Jews seized by the Arrow Cross.

Still the noose tightened around us. On November 8, 1944, the government crowded more than 70,000 Jews into the Ujlaki brickyards—about the size of a city block. As winter approached, they began the notorious forced march to labor camps in Austria. Thousands of Hungarian Jews died of exposure, starvation, fatigue and disease. Thousands more were shot because they were too slow, too old, too young or too weak to walk.

The remaining Jews of Budapest were ordered into a closed ghetto centered on Dohany Street. Lutz immediately added another 76 safe houses. Almost 25,000 Jews were stuffed into difficult and crowded conditions, but at least they assumed they'd be safe while the war raged on. They were fed and sustained out of the meager resources of the Consulate and whatever they'd managed to conserve. The Sterns and others somehow produced 15,000 meals a week for the starving community as well.

The Glass House held an estimated 3,000 Jews. During the day, when the building functioned as the Swiss Legation, Jews hid in the tunnels under the building. At night, it became a beehive of hidden people.

As my father and mother had before them, the Sterns protected me by keeping me ignorant about what was going on. They kept their thoughts and the tensions of daily life to themselves, shielding me as best they could. Yes, I was aware that the restaurant was no longer thriving, that it was, in fact, closed to all but a few people on all but few days. I knew that school, which opened briefly in the fall, had quickly closed.

Using false papers, Bubi, at age 13, left for Mandate Palestine right after the High Holy Days. I was bound to him heart and soul, and now he was leaving for an unknown destination. I was heartbroken because I was so attached to him. I stayed with him every moment as he prepared for his journey, and he allowed me to stick to him because he knew that this separation was very different.

Turi, too, was soon gone, sent back to the Rombach Synagogue, which had been converted into a holding center for children.

I realized that our lives had changed, that the joy was gone, and that my dolls, fun, and other luxuries had vanished. We were "trapped" between the apartment and the courtyard, except for my occasional forays to the outside.

The Sterns, as connected as they were to everything in the community, had to be aware of the activities at the Glass House from the very beginning—or at least since 1942. It's easy to assume that my *Apu* knew Carl Lutz; I am convinced Lutz frequented Stern's restaurant in the old days, along with the rest of Budapest's café society.

The Sterns always knew everything there was to know about everybody and what was happening in the city and so I am sure they knew about the Swiss Legation, what the Red Cross was up to, and what Wallenberg was doing. I believe that Stern, like my father, had long plotted to stay one step ahead of disaster to keep his family safe. And he and Ilonka did a wonderful job for as long as they could.

When the ghetto was established, we were already in it. We never left the apartment again, until the three of us—Marci, Ilonka Stern and I—moved into the Glass House sometime in November 1944. Bella stayed behind with the Goldbergers.

The Sterns knew that I needed their reassurance as the terror began to set in. Knowing that I was already upset because I had to leave my familiar surroundings, *Apu* took me on his knee to explain what was happening. He gently told me why it was important for us to go into hiding in the Glass House and asked me not to worry, for he would keep me safe at his side.

I remember the Glass House as a huge, warehouse-like place surrounding a spacious courtyard open to the sky. There was a kitchen on the ground floor, with a wooden worktable in the middle of the room, a very large stove, and a large pantry. The kitchen opened onto the courtyard, and these two spaces—kitchen and courtyard—became very familiar to me.

Jews were not allowed to have radios, but there was one in the kitchen at the Glass House, and people were always huddled around it, trying to make sense of the broadcasts, wondering if and when the Allies would make it to Budapest. Hope of liberation was but a flicker in their hearts.

My *Anyu*, because she knew how to run a major restaurant, was in charge of the kitchen, and spent much of her time there. The courtyard was the only place to find fresh air, which we did mostly at night—and very quietly. We were, after all, in hiding. During the day, we lived in tunnels underneath the building. It was very cold down there, colder even than the courtyard, so we spent lots of our time huddling together for warmth. But even with blankets, warm clothing and the radiant heat of other bodies, I was never warm enough.

The tunnels were narrow and dark. Most of the time we sat against the damp stone walls, with our feet planted on the cold stone floor. And when your feet are cold, your whole body stays cold. If we wanted to, we could walk around and even play in a few areas where the tunnel widened out. I vaguely remember games of hopscotch and marbles—but we had to watch the noise, since we never knew when Nazi or Arrow Cross officials were visiting the Legation upstairs. At night, when the offices were closed and the staff was gone, the women would head up to the kitchen to prepare meals under *Anyu's* direction, while the children were sent out to the courtyard to let off some steam. I loved to spend my time with *Anyu* in the kitchen, where the big, commercial stove was powerful enough to heat the whole room and I could stay warm and cozy.

Most of the food we ate came from cans, and one evening, when I was helping out, someone asked me to check on the food in the oven. I did not realize the oven was hot and that there were unopened cans of food inside. When I opened the door there was a sudden bang, a whoosh and a steaming cloud of hot food exploded in my face, unto my clothes and all over the kitchen. The scalding muck seared my face and I screamed in shock and pain. A doctor was sent for immediately to tend to my face and prevent scarring for life.

Someone had put cans in the oven to heat, but hadn't punctured them to let the steam out. To this day I am convinced that the culprit, who never came forward to take responsibility, was some upper-class woman, clueless about cooking, who had never seen the inside of a stove until she came to the Glass House. She clearly didn't realize that in a hot oven the steam would build up inside until the can exploded with the force of a grenade!

The aftereffects of those exploding canned goods really hurt me; it took weeks for me to heal and months for the scars to disappear. But the canned goods were also lifesavers; they were our only source of nutrition. When Soviet troops placed Budapest under siege on Christmas Eve 1944, they cut the food supplies, the electricity, gas and water. These canned goods stood between us and starvation. Ever my guardian, *Anyu* always made sure there was extra food for me.

Somehow people managed to survive. They drew water from wells and even one of the *mikvahs* (the ritual baths), burned wood (lots of furniture) and coal for fuel. For the Jews, already hiding in various safe houses, these were relatively minor privations.

In the meantime, the Arrow Cross thugs violated diplomatic immunity all over the city by raiding the safe houses and grabbing whomever they could. Lutz and other diplomats dashed from safe house to safe house to maintain security. Lutz's protests to the Szalasi government brought promises of protection, but the government did not control the *Nyilas*, who grew ever more vicious as the Red Army approached. It was as if the monsters needed to suck out the last ounce of Jewish lifeblood before they themselves expired.

On the afternoon of December 31, 1944, the *Nyilas* came to the Glass House to quench that bloody thirst and celebrate the New Year by murdering Jews. Their motorcycles roared up Vadasz Street, brakes screeching. We heard the steel heels of their boots clanging on the pavement. One of our men grabbed the telephone and made a frantic call.

"Quickly!" he shouted into the handset. "The *Nyilas* are here! The police are letting them in! They are taking us and will shoot us outside. Help us! Hurry!"

Just then the *Nyilas* crashed through the door with rifles raised and shot him. He dropped the phone as he died.

They searched the building and found all of us hiding in the tunnels. We were herded out into the gray, cold street. I was with *Apu*. *Anyu* was in the kitchen with several women and a few children, locked in the darkened pantry, where they tried to remain absolutely still. In the street, there was chaos. The *Nyilas* were shouting curses and orders. The Jews were crying out in surprise and fear. I was so frightened, I begged *Apu* to lift me in his arms and hold me, but he didn't have the strength. Instead he calmed me with his voice and took my hand in his.

The enemy ordered us to line up. They pistol-whipped crying children and several of the grownups. We all grew quiet. Then, in an orderly fashion, Arrow Cross troopers began to work their way down the line, shooting people, one by one, one bullet at a time.

Unlike the wholesale, assemblyline murders in the gas chambers or shootings by *Einzatzgruppen*, Hitler's mobile killing troops, this killing was very personal. Our killers looked right into our eyes so we could see exactly who and what they were: ugly-souled men with guns who allowed power and greed to run amok. Contaminated by jealous hatred, now we, innocent and unarmed, would die from what infected them.

I held tight to *Apu's* hand, that big, strong hand that meant safety and security to me. But with certain death staring us in the face, even *Apu* was trembling. Still, it was my fear that concerned him most. "Don't be frightened," he whispered to me, "Don't be scared," he said, his voice cracking.

I heard the murders take place, one shot at a time. Neatly. Carefully. With almost delicate deliberation, each shot brought the killing closer to *Apu* and to me. I tried to hide behind *Apu*, clutching his leg and his coat. And suddenly, I began to think: "How will I escape? Where can I hide? How will I survive?"

I could not stop my tears, and my mind went back to the Žilina train station on the day my family was taken away. Then, the sense of a greater power, the same power that I felt when I fell into the latrine, washed over me once more. Though I was frightened more than I ever was before, the feeling infused me with a fierce desire to live. "I know," I thought. "When they get to me, I'll fall down with the dead bodies around me and make believe I've already been shot. That way, they won't kill me, and they won't know I am alive."

But when I heard the screams of the dying, and as the shots came closer, I wet myself and could feel the warm liquid spreading through my thick tights as it ran down my legs. I was shivering but I said nothing to *Apu*, I only held his hand tighter and snuggled closer to his side.

All of a sudden, a Red Cross vehicle careened around the corner and burst into the street, disgorging Swiss Red Cross officials and members of the Swiss diplomatic corps as it screeched to a halt. The officials waved papers at the Arrow Cross and yelled at the top of their lungs, "Stop shooting! Stop the killing! Stop! Now!"

Just like that, it was over. The presence of the diplomats was enough to halt wholesale murder. It seemed that even Arrow Cross thugs knew they couldn't shoot internationally protected diplomats. With the vicious roar of their motorcycle engines echoing in our ears, the foiled murderers took off like bats from Hell. Stunned, incredulous, having escaped murder by moments, we slowly piled back into the Glass House. A great quiet settled over us, as if God Himself had silenced those guns.

And then came the weeping, the mourning, and the cries of pain and relief that wracked the building for the rest of the night and beyond.

Later we learned from Baruch Leibovic, a community leader, that the desperate phone call from the dead man had been heard. David Friedman, a leader in the Mizrachi movement, took the call. Leibovic watched Friedman's face turn white, then gray as he listened to what was going on at the other end of the line. When it went dead, Friedman called the others for help.

After the war, *Anyu* told a story that compounded the tragedy of that dreadful night. By that time, there was no longer a need to hide the truth from me. I was no longer a child. I was a witness to cold-blooded murder, no longer an innocent. *Anyu* told us how, as the women and children hid in the pantry, a crying baby threatened to give them all away. The baby's distraught mother didn't know what to do. "I'll take the baby," said one of the other women. She took the child, and turned her back on the mother in the dark pantry. Holding the child close to her body, she clasped the infant tighter and tighter—until the baby could never cry again.

Of everything my *Anyu* saw and heard and suffered during the war and after it, nothing affected her as much as that baby's death. As strong as she was, it was clear this incident had shaken her to the core and had rattled her faith and her health.

I do not know how many people died that bloody night at the Glass House. From March 19, 1944 until January 1945, the Germans and their Hungarian collaborators destroyed 560,000 Jews. They were murdered or died of starvation and disease in the camps and ghettos. But numbers are only that. Numbers. And numbers lose their meaning if we forget that each number is a soul, a person, a potentiality. Of the 700,000+ Jews who celebrated New Year's Day 1944 in Hungary, only a small remnant survived a year later. I was part of that remnant.

In January 1945, the sounds of the big guns booming in the distance became a constant noise and the spark of our hope flared anew. Soon we could hear sustained gunfire from machine guns and rifles on the local streets. Was it possible that the Soviets had broken through to Pest?

We emerged cautiously from the Glass House, worried that we were being drawn into a trap. But when we confirmed that the Red Army was in the city, the Sterns led us back to 10 Rombach Street, dancing all the way, kissing our liberators when they saw them.

From every nook and cranny of Pest, Jews emerged from the shadows, weeping with joy. The anxiety and dread that had weighed on us for so many years was lifted at last and we could taste freedom on our lips.

But it wasn't over just yet. The January 18th liberation of Pest, on the east side of the Danube, was stage one of the battle for the city. It took another month of bloody fighting before the Germans in Buda surrendered, and on February 13 the Soviet flag finally flew over Budapest.

Once again, God had saved me from unspeakable carnage. It had to mean something, but I didn't yet know what that was.

CHAPTER SEVEN
Liberation

It was a bittersweet time. Though the existential threat to the Jews was officially over, no one had realized just how staggering the losses were. Coping with those losses—taken from the perspective of personal, not communal losses—rebuilding one's life was a daunting prospect, especially when the betrayals and murders of our families were often committed by neighbors and "friends."

I knew the war was over, but I didn't understand anything else about it. I had no idea that there had been millions of Jews murdered. I understood, but could not accept, that Mama, Papa, Robi and Rena were dead and I would never see them again. I knew our enemies seethed with unrestricted hatred for the Jewish people, a hatred that still simmers today, all over the world, even where there are no Jews, causing many Jews to feel that they are still not entirely safe—anywhere.

What I knew then was that I was once more ensconced with the Sterns, with my *Anyu* and *Apu* at 10 Rumbach. The building had been spared destruction and was still home to the Schwartzes and the Goldbergers. But the men of the house—the husbands who had been taken to slave labor camps or deported—never came home again.

Turi and Bella survived as well, and I was reunited with them. I was overjoyed. Bella had stayed behind on Rumbach Street with the Schwartzes while we hid in the Glass House. Turi had stayed at the Rumbach Street Synagogue, where the transit camp/prison had been turned into a youth camp. Bubi, in the meantime, was making his way to Palestine as per the instructions from the Belzer Rebbe but had been detoured through Romania before he could get to to the new Jewish homeland. I missed him most of all.

With Bella after the war in Budapest.

As a child with childish dreams, I assumed things would go back to normal, to golden days of play and parties, new clothes and new shoes, school and friends, and bright celebrations at the restaurant, restored once again to its pre-war splendor. But it never happened. Nothing was the same again.

The Jewish community of Budapest was broken, its traditions smashed, its institutions crippled or destroyed. Stern's Restaurant, once a vibrant magnet for the capital's prominent citizens, struggled to survive; *Apu* was barely able to keep it afloat. School resumed slowly and shakily; there were very few teachers left after the war. My friends' parents were eager to begin new lives in new countries with what was left of their families. We Mannheimers would be on the move as well.

Soon, my siblings and I were separated. Bella, now a tall, thin teenager, went to our Aunt Mela in Békéscaba, who hired tutors to provide her with the schooling she had missed. From there she was sent to Vienna, where Aliyah Bet, the Zionist group that had smuggled people into Mandate Palestine since the mid-1930s, brought her to Trieste with other children who had survived the war. Through the illegal immigration underground network, Aliyah Bet gathered survivors in port cities on the Mediterranean and put them aboard converted freighters and fishing boats, many of them barely seaworthy, to take them to the Jewish Homeland.

Turi, as well, became involved with Aliyah Bet and was soon on a ship headed for Haifa. Unfortunately, the ship was intercepted by the British, who put him into one of their Displaced Persons camps in Cyprus. These camps were surrounded by barbed wire but were not at all like the camps in Europe. They offered vocational training, Hebrew language and Judaism courses. There he remained locked up until 1947, when he was allowed to go to Mandate Palestine.

My world was as insecure as ever; it began to crack in earnest when my beloved *Anyu* fell victim to an illness that began to consume her when we were still in the Glass House. Once we returned to Rumbach Street, dark foreboding gripped my heart when *Anyu* became very sick indeed. Though she remained beautiful and unchanging at first, I could sense the diminution of her energy, the ebbing of her vitality.

Within months, she was bedridden—the cancer must have been very aggressive—and I made sure I spent time with her in our big bedroom, though I didn't quite know how to amuse her. I knew something was very wrong, but didn't understand it. And while *Anyu* was always happy to see me, always loving and tender, her discomfort and fatigue were evident. She would rally when I entered the room—I wonder now how much strength that cost her—but she tired easily, and I would sit quietly at her bedside, holding her hand while she dozed. It made me very uncomfortable to sit with her, and I was impatient to leave.

Apu became very sad and withdrawn. Everyone noticed that the spirited man they looked up to had become a lonely, bewildered creature unable and unwilling to connect. Though he still held me in his arms as I loved to be held, he was distracted—the joy and fun were gone, never to return.

Still there were a few happy moments that spring. On May 1, the Communist holiday, there was a great celebration honoring the coming of spring and the value of labor. Like everyone else in Budapest, we hung red banners from the window and watched Red Army troops, reeling with drink, parade past our building. Seven days later, Germany surrendered to the Allies, the war against the Jews was officially over, and new chapters of Jewish life in what was to become the State of Israel and America were opening.

In the Stern's apartment, a bittersweet chapter was coming to an end. One day the Sterns' surviving relatives came to see *Anyu*. I was bewildered by the visit. There was no holiday; there was no birthday, nothing to celebrate. Why were they all there?

Now I understand that they'd come to say farewell to a wonderful woman who was on the threshold to the next world. Everyone but me knew *Anyu* was terminally ill and that nothing more could be done. They came into the bedroom and arranged themselves at her bedside so that she could touch each one in turn. It was her way of saying goodbye.

After that she faded quickly as the disease turned her into a skeletal caricature of herself. My beautiful angel, my protector, my loving *Anyu* had disappeared. And so, child that I was—understanding nothing—I withdrew from her, afraid of what she had become, unwilling to touch the hand I had once clasped so lovingly.

One gray day *Apu*, his face masked with grief, took me into his arms and weeping bitter tears, gently and in a broken voice said, "She is no longer with us. She has died."

I began to sob uncontrollably. Relatives and friends who'd come to stand last watch were also crying and, much as they tried, they were unable to comfort me.

Ilonka Stern was a woman whose loving embrace had gathered me to her when I needed it most. She became my mother, and I lost that love again. The arms of those who tried to comfort me on that day seemed counterfeit to me.

I don't remember the funeral. Perhaps I was not allowed to attend because of my young age. Perhaps I did go and the trauma wiped out the memory of it. Imagine a child who at a tender age had already lost two mothers; a father and two siblings. I was devastated.

To help me deal with my grief, or perhaps because he could not cope with raising a child who served as a living reminder of his beloved Ilonka, *Apu* sent me to a children's camp in the Hungarian hills. It clearly was not healthy for me to be in the apartment watching *Apu* wander through the rooms like a lost soul. Sending me to a place where I could be with other children seemed like a good idea, so off I went.

It was simply awful, the worst place in the world for a spoiled child like me. The facilities were spartan, the food inedible—a situation that exacerbated my misery for having to be there in the first place. Some girls were mean, others were bullies. Some were just uninteresting. When I thought things would get better, they didn't. Sadness engulfed me.

In desperation I attached myself to one of the older campers who also hated the place. Though she was four or five years older than I was, she was miserable, too, so we commiserated. When she heard how badly I wanted to go home, she suggested we abandon the camp; that we run away together, since she knew the way to Budapest. And that is precisely what we did.

On a sunny, balmy, bright day, when no one was paying attention to us, we sneaked out of the camp. If we heard someone coming, we would get off the road and hide. This teenager really did know the route to Budapest, and our trip took just a couple of days. She was also smart enough to make sure we had food, blankets and some money.

Traveling by bus and on foot, we followed country roads and sometimes cut across fields. I know we slept, but I can't remember where. Astonishingly, we succeeded in making our way back to Budapest, arriving in the city just as a torrential summer storm broke and swirled about us. How we did it remains a faint memory, details escape me, but I do remember arriving at 10 Rumbach to the sound of thunder, soaking wet, with blisters on my feet and canker sores on my face. I ached all over and must have been a sight, but I can't say for sure. As soon as the apartment door was opened, I passed out on the hallway floor.

Apu was frantic from the moment the camp staff called him and told him that I had disappeared. Though he was overjoyed to see me, he was angry with me at the same time. All of that negative emotion must have evaporated, however, when I collapsed on his doorstep. I wouldn't know since I was out for days. Running away from that dreadful camp was a desperate act that had sapped my physical and emotional strength. I was exhausted, and before I could recover from my adventure, the traumas of my wartime experiences finally caught up with me and I became seriously ill.

The months of running from place to place in Slovakia while my parents tried to save us; the separation from my siblings as we were scattered around the countryside to escape the Hlinka Guard; the winter trek to Budapest from Nitra; my experience in the Conti Street prison and the Glass House, all of this topped off by the death of Ilonka Stern and my exile to that disgusting summer camp, had taken their toll. I just fell apart.

For weeks I woke feverish, screaming in fear and soaked in sweat from dreadful nightmares that attacked me in the dead of night. In each dream I was hunted; soldiers chased me; Hlinka Guards and Nazis held me down as I screamed to be let go; people climbed through windows to take us all away. I would sit bolt upright in the bed I shared with Ilonka's niece, Frieda Goldberger. And night after night, Frieda would gently wash me down with cool water to bring down the fever, calming me back to sleep.

Though the Glass House was a safe house, it seems that its chilly, dank tunnels had done their insidious work. I developed a persistent upper-respiratory infection that steadily grew worse. My body raged with high fevers, as Frieda tried to help me however she could.

Preoccupied as he was with his own grief and with the restaurant, *Apu* still found moments here and there to look in on me and shower me with affection. He also had the best doctors in Budapest on call for me. More than anything, he wished I would get well, to go back to being the lovely little light of his heart.

It took a few weeks for the fever to go down. I still remained very weak and frail. The doctor also discovered scar tissue on my lung, probably from an undiagnosed disease I caught in the Glass House tunnels. It was going to be a long recovery, requiring complete bed rest.

Frieda set up a couch for me in the parlor so that I could still be part of family life while recuperating. From then on, that became my space. Soon I began eating—fluids at first. Someone went to the milkmaid each morning to fetch the fresh milk the doctor said was essential to my recovery. For the rest of that summer I lay on the couch drinking milk and eating whatever was put in front of me, as Frieda *Néni* and one of the maids slowly nursed me back to health. Frieda's daughter, Judit, was my constant companion, and so was Riki Schwartz, Baba *Néni*'s son. Other children in the building would come to visit, too, saving me from boredom. One girl in particular, who was not Jewish, spent lots of time playing with me. There was no television in those days, no CDs, no DVDs. You learned to amuse yourself by reading lots of books or playing with your dolls.

At one point, I was sent to a hotel-sanitarium in the rolling hills on the Buda side of the river. It was a pretty spot with stunning views of the Danube. The staff would put me in a lounge chair on a grassy knoll surrounded by woods dotted with summer villas and cottages. The green grass was scattered with vivid yellow buttercups and dandelions. I would sit there for hours, staring at the river, or watching the clouds float by in the bright blue sky, letting my imagination work on the shapes. Sometimes, someone would come and read to me, but it was all very boring, albeit peaceful, and it helped me recover.

CHAPTER EIGHT
Goodbye to Budapest

My illness was not the only summer surprise of 1945. *Apu* was introduced to a woman. I know nothing about her except that something began to happen between them and that she had no interest in children. Before long, I understood this woman was nothing like my beloved *Anyu*.

In the meantime, my recovery was a slow one. As summer faded to fall, I was still not well enough to go to school, so I lay on the couch while a tutor went over our lessons. The doctor would shake his head in dissatisfaction each time he examined me and suggested that perhaps it would be better for my health if I left Budapest for the mountains, where the fresh air was supposed to improve the conditions of those suffering from lung ailments.

Of course I didn't want to go, but by late fall I couldn't wait to get out of the apartment. *Apu*, unfortunately for me, remarried. Naively I assumed that *Apu*'s new wife would love me the way *Anyu* had, but since I was not *Apu*'s "real" child she disdained my presence

The High Tatras.

and made it clear that she wanted me gone. I felt her contempt and shied away from her and, as a result, from my beloved *Apu*. That's when he decided to send me to the High Tatra mountains.

For the life of me even now I cannot fathom why *Apu* married such a selfish woman. After a horrendous war that destroyed just about everything anyone had known and loved, on the heels of Jewish losses that compounded the destruction a thousand-fold, it is natural to reach out for companionship as you try to start your life over, especially someone who was *Apu's* age. I could easily understand his need for a companion and someone to care for him. But that such a cold woman had succeeded *Anyu* was incomprehensible to a seven-year-old.

Today I believe that *Apu* was torn in two by his wife's attitude. The doctor's suggestion, then recommendation, then insistence that I be sent up to the mountains for clean air was the workable solution to an untenable situation. Yes, *Apu* loved me—of this I have not the slightest doubt—but he had staked his future on that woman and was greatly taken with her. No doubt he could have resisted her increasingly insistent declarations that he not be burdened with a "stranger's" child, but if he could persuade himself that I needed to leave—and I did need to go—he could assuage his sense of guilt.

I myself was of two minds. The woman sent clear signals that I was not welcome or wanted, and the marriage underscored that. Being sent to the mountains "for my health" sounded an awful lot like being "shipped out." On the other hand, I understood that I needed to get well, and I wanted to be away from the new Mrs. Stern as keenly as she wanted me gone. That blunted the pain of rejection, and it was easier to say goodbye.

When *Apu* wished me farewell, he held me on his lap for a long time, hugged me close, cuddled me as he always had, and told me how much he loved me. "That's why I want you to go to the mountains," he said, "so you can grow healthy again." It made sense to him, and it suddenly made sense to me, too. He also reassured me that when I was better, I would come back to him. *Apu* had researched the best places for my recovery, made the arrangements, and sometime in the winter of 1945-1946, I went up into the High Tatras, a mountain range in what was once again Czechoslovakia.

Judith in the High Tatras.

Once he and the new Mrs. Stern put me on the train, I never saw *Apu* again. What's worse is that to this day I have no idea what happened to him. When I was older I did try to find out, but the trail had gotten cold.

The Tatras are the highest range in the Carpathian Mountains, linking the Balkans with the Alps. Its northernmost ridge boasts peaks nearly 9,000 feet high. It was my fortune to be sent to Vysoke Tatra, a region sparsely populated to this day. It's a mecca for hikers, skiers, and other vacationers, as well the traditional site of sanatoria for the treatment of respiratory diseases.

I was glad to get away from *Apu*'s new wife, but I very much regretted leaving *Apu* himself and missed him terribly. Still, it was a new beginning for me, and I could take advantage of it. I had never been in the mountains before, and what I saw enchanted and excited me.

Everything around me looked like picture postcards from a fantastical winter wonderland. The thick green branches of the evergreen forests that lined the slopes were bowed under the weight of crystal white snow. They looked as if an expert baker had frosted them with the most delicious white icing. The tall snow-covered trees looked stunning against the cloudless azure sky. Where there were no trees, there were towering slabs of black granite and gray limestone, strewn across the top of the world by icy glaciers—interrupted here and there by icy sparkling waterfalls that froze in the cold and looked like gargantuan icicles. It truly was a wonder, and the air smelled deliciously clean.

I was met at the station and taken by car to Villa Sylvia. There was also another villa, called Erika. Both villas had been hotels before the war and were turned into children's healthcare facilities by the American Jewish Joint Distribution Committee (JDC), an organization that collected money to help Jewish people everywhere. After the war they concentrated on helping Holocaust survivors, especially orphans.

Villa Sylvia was a plain, big, white stucco house, two stories tall, with the public rooms — like the dining hall — downstairs and the dorm rooms upstairs. It was surrounded by a large lawn that was covered with snow when I got there. I was warmly welcomed and noticed that the resident children came in all shapes, ages and sizes. Some, like me, were orphans. The people on staff, nurses and teachers, were under the management of the JDC. A doctor was always on call. Most of the children were subsidized by donations to Jewish organizations. I think *Apu* may have helped. After they examined me, the staff showed me to my assigned bed on the second floor.

I instantly felt at home. After the sadness of my last months in Budapest, the children's center was heaven. I loved being surrounded by the forest, and I embraced my residency happily. I liked to help the little children with their lessons and games. At mealtimes, we all sat together at long tables, but I did notice that no one observed *Shabbat* and no one seemed to care.

On visiting days, children whose parents came to see them would "visit" me too and invite me to join their families for day trips. This was a very heartwarming effort on their part, and I always enjoyed myself. Still, I knew I was an orphan and my friends had their parents when I had none, so there was always loneliness in my soul.

Everyone was unconditionally kind. In class, it didn't matter how old we were, we were all in it together and helped each other. Our medical treatments were working and we all slowly improved. People liked me, grownups and children alike. Once the staff saw how much I enjoyed playing with the younger children, they pressed me into service as an aide. I loved it and welcomed the responsibility. I was also flattered by the affection of the little ones; it was good for me to feel loved again.

The cold, crisp, clean mountain air was the key to our medical treatment. When I'd first arrived, its fresh-tasting thinness made me dizzy. I loved the air's pungent piney edge and sucked in great gulps of it, but the reduced oxygen at that altitude would cause me to faint. In time, I grew accustomed to the thinner air and participated fully in the round of daily activities the staff scheduled for us.

There were outings to a nearby lake for ice skating, and there were skiing lessons on the "bunny slopes" at one of the nearby ski resorts. At the villa we built snowmen and pitched snowballs at one another. As winter waned, there were bracing hikes into the fragrant woods to visit shining ice caves and, when spring came, we climbed mountain trails leading as high as we could go without special equipment.

Gentian and campanula grew among the rocks on the slopes; we walked on carpets of soft pine needles that took years to create and ate lunch in the cooling spray of tumbling waterfalls. We picked flowers, gathered mushrooms and wild strawberries and brought them back to the villa to feast on. Our miserable memories were beginning to fade as we concentrated on having fun and living fully.

On one of our spring hikes, we learned a lesson about the dangers that can be hidden in beauty — sort of like the new Mrs. Stern, I thought. A young girl ate a poison mushroom, became deathly ill and had to be rushed back to the villa to get her stomach pumped. My fleeting hope was that *Apu* shouldn't suffer dangers from the beauty he married, and I sometimes wondered what happened to them after I left.

But not for a moment did the episode of the poison mushroom stifle my enjoyment of the outdoor life. The treatment was working. Time in the mountains unleashed the energetic, sports-loving child within the traumatized city kid. I reveled in the activity, loved the majestic mountains and was happy living in the children's center.

Relatives I had never met before were dispatched to see me by my Aunt Giska, who still lived on the estate in Nitra. She was the ever-benevolent overseer of my whereabouts and well being. Sometimes, not often, *Apu's* friends brought me gifts and candy treats or took me skiing.

These friends of his would be in the mountains on holiday with their families and would take me to the steeper slopes where they skied with their children. But none of them ever offered to let me ski those grownup trails, and I felt that it somehow meant I wasn't worthy of careening down the ski runs with their families. Decades later I did indeed ski the big mountains, and enjoyed it as much as I had imagined I would when I was a child.

I was speaking Czech again. At first, I stumbled a bit, but in no time my mother tongue returned to me with perfect fluency. I was back in my native land, not far from my roots. Of course, I dreamed that my parents were coming to get me, to take me back—to take all of us back—to the normal life into which I had been born. I knew, logically, that that was not going to happen. But dreams are dreams.

In the meantime, Aunt Giska, as always, kept track of my movements and tabs on my situation. Because she couldn't travel far, and I was too young to go to Nitra by myself, she and I would meet periodically in the Piešťany railroad station, a practical solution to a thorny problem. I'd get on a train from the High Tatras, while Aunt Giska would catch her train in Nitra. We would both get off in Piešťany. I would spend the ride gazing through the window at the sun-dappled fields, meadows and forests, enjoying the view.

Aunt Giska, who always wore the same black outfit and never seemed to age, always got there first and would sit on a bench in the station and wait for me. In greeting me, she gave me no hugs but did kiss me on the cheek. As a reserved Victorian-style woman, she never was demonstrative, but I knew she cared about me deeply.

As we sat in the station, I would report the latest news from school, and, after she asked me if I needed anything she could bring to our next meeting, she would give me a "care" package filled with baked goods, candies and other treats to take back to the home.

For my Aunt Giska, the past was a country she did not want to visit, so we never spoke of it. She didn't want me wandering around in places that would evoke bitter and frightening memories. We never ventured out of the station. There were no side-trips to the house on Stefanikova Street, to the benches along the river or the crystal bridge. There were too many memories in the center of that town for either of us to bear.

In the fall of 1946, the staff at the JDC children's center determined that I was well enough to leave. Aunt Giska met me at the Pieštany station. The meeting took place while Eva Steiner, my best friend, and I were transferring from the train that was taking us from the sanitarium in the high

Eva Steiner.

High Tatras to Nove Mesto, where there was an orphanage run by one of the Jewish organizations. I could never find out if that school was run by the JDC,

Youth Aliyah (an Israeli Zionist organization) or the World Jewish Congress.

"You'll like it there," Aunt Giska told me during our hurried visit. "There will be lots of children there."

Nove Mesto is a small town that sits on the banks of the Vaha River — the very same river on which both Pieštany and Žilina sit, a river that seemed to course through my early life. In fact, Nove Mesto was about ten miles from Pieštany, but it was a universe away from the life I had known there.

Nove Mesto Town Center.

Jews had lived in Nove Mesto since 1689. When the synagogue was built in 1780, it became the second largest Jewish community in the region. The town's 1,500 Jews were all deported during the Holocaust. Less than one hundred of the town's Jews came back to discover that the synagogue was destroyed and their community was lost.

The school, run by a couple named Vogel/Fogel, was an orphanage really, and before the war had been Ohel David, the Jewish community's old age home. It was a stone house with a small yard that sat just across the road from a convent with a Catholic school. All the "students" at our school were orphans, all of us victims of the Holocaust, all of us survivors from somewhere else.

I cannot remember how many children were there with me. I do remember that we ranged in age from the very young to young adults. Eva Steiner, who had been my friend at Villa Sylvia, had no idea where she came from, no memory of her parents, no ties to anyone except for an aunt and uncle who had survived the war—her only links to an otherwise invisible past. As a result, she relied on our friendship and grew dependent on me. I responded in kind, not because it was flattering, which it was, but because I needed and wanted a friend as much as she did. We were inseparable. We shared clothes and secrets and seemed to think alike in every way. Two souls set adrift, brutally cut off from our roots, we clung to one another and helped each other turn our faces to the future—we created a friendship that has lasted a lifetime.

The Vogels/Fogels were a warm and wonderful couple who loved us and took good care of us. They had a chicken coop in the back yard, and each morning one of our chores was to gather eggs for breakfast. A small vegetable garden supplemented our meager food allowance and provided a source of fresh nutrition. But feeding us placed a strain on the budget allocated for our care. There was not enough reserve for our education, so when the nuns offered to let us attend their Catholic School for free, the Vogels/Fogels jumped at the chance.

In exchange, we were required to attend daily Mass and listen to minor but persistent Catholic proselytizing. Every day I lined up with the other children to enter the church. I duly took my place in the pew and knelt when the rest of the congregation did. Though it bothered me, when I knew the nuns' eyes were on me, I would even cross myself—something I thought was fun to do. But the nuns were kind, and even if they thought we were possible converts or future nuns and priests, I still appreciated their compassion. I wanted them to know that and I wanted them to like me, and so I knelt before the crucifix and crossed myself in the name of the Father, the Son and the Holy Ghost. While I went through the motions in the chapel, my heart knew they were empty gestures, born of a child's desire to be accepted.

I also realized I was vulnerable, and who knows what might have happened if I had forgotten my own past? I wasn't yet strong enough to stand on my Judaism and battle the faith the nuns offered. If I would have needed to convert to survive, I would have. Under the circumstances, I didn't have to.

CHAPTER NINE
The Kindertransport

In the winter of 1947-48, Rabbi Dr. Solomon Schonfeld, a rescue activist in England, returned to Europe to search for Jewish children. Immediately before and during the war, Rabbi Schonfeld had been responsible for organizing *Kindertransports*, literally shipments of children, that brought thousands of Jewish children to the United Kingdom from Europe. For this last official *Kindertransport*, he had permits for 148 orphans. When desperate parents, who wanted to provide their children with some sort of positive future heard what he was doing, they begged him to give the orphans' permits to their own children. He could not refuse.

Why be surprised? For the Jews, after the war, Europe was a gargantuan graveyard, where every step you took squeezed blood from the ground. The antisemitism that allowed Nazi regimes to flourish across the continent remained rooted in its soil, and while the Communists who conquered the eastern provinces and countries promised tolerance, lost freedom and criminalization of individual enterprise was the price the masses paid. Everyone wanted out — grownups and children alike. They pleaded with Schonfeld, "Take our children to England. Take them to a new land far away from here. Give them a fresh start, set them on a new path in life. Give them freedom to grow up, and we will follow later."

Yenko Katscher was very persuasive. Yenko and Schonfeld had been students together in Nitra, both close with the rescue activist from Nitra, Rabbi Weissmandl of the Working Group. When Schonfeld arrived in Nitra after the war, Yenko convinced Schonfeld to take his children, Ivan and Anni, to England, too. Yenko also told the good rabbi about me — the orphan Judith Mannheimer, the little slip of a girl who had been through so much. By the time Dr. Schonfeld arrived to search for Jewish orphans in the convent at Nove Mesto, my name was already etched in his mind.

Dr. Schonfeld reminded me at once of my *Apu* Stern. As soon as I saw him, I responded to him in much the same way I reacted to *Apu* when I'd first arrived at his home in Budapest. In both cases, I knew that if I was unable to articulate my thoughts, they would still understand me and get me whatever I needed to survive, and more. "Here is help; this man means to do me good."

In both cases, my intuition was correct.

Schonfeld looked like a younger version of Maurice Stern: the same robust build, the same intense blue eyes, and in Schonfeld's case, a square beard that was reddish-blond, not gray. When he spoke to me, Schonfeld focused on me so intently — his eyes were so passionate and full of sympathy — that I never felt alone in his presence. From the very beginning, the good doctor made me feel special. Perhaps he

Rabbi Dr. Solomon Schonfeld.

made every child feel special, but it didn't matter. As long as he made me feel safe and good about myself, I was very happy.

He found me in the orphanage in Nove Mesto, where everything had already been arranged with Aunt Giska and the authorities. I was going to England and that was that. The die had been cast. Nothing would seem familiar to me ever again. I was embarking on an adventure in what seemed like a new dimension, out of the world I had known since birth.

When my friend Eva heard the news, it struck her like a body blow. She sobbed uncontrollably, and her tears drew an instant question from the rabbi.

"Why are you crying?" he asked.

As the tears rolled down her rosy cheeks, and her chest heaved with her sobs, Eva gulped out, "Because my best friend is leaving; because we share everything;

because Judith taught me the *Sh'ma Yisrael* prayer and she is the only connection I have to *Yiddishkeit* (Judaism). She said I should learn the prayer and that saying it would give me strength."

It happened to be true. I taught Eva the *Sh'ma* because I truly felt that way about it. It was one of the few vestiges of Judaism that had remained with me after God had intervened and saved me. Quietly reciting the *Sh'ma* in bed each night was a great comfort to me and a source of strength and inspiration. It was almost automatic — the typical way children say their bedtime prayers. Though I didn't understand the theology or the significance of the prayer, I knew it was the central prayer of Judaism and, since it made me feel safe in God's hands, when I said it I felt I was conversing with Him.

That nightly recitation of the *Sh'ma* affirmed my connections to members of my family, living and dead, and to the history of the Jewish people. Now I realize I was maintaining the continuity of an ancient heritage that had belonged to my mother and father; it also belonged to me and I was to pass it on to my descendants.

Eva, who could not remember ever being taught anything about Judaism, loved to recite the prayer with me. What neither of us realized was just how much that story resonated with Rabbi Dr. Schonfeld. This was the last *Kindertransport* he could take out of Europe. The Iron Curtain was falling around him as he swept through Central Europe searching for Jewish children to rescue. He walked through dormitories at convents

The last post-war *Kindertransport*.

and monasteries, after the priests and nuns had assured him that there were no Jewish children in those beds. When he passed by each bed, he murmured the *Sh'ma*, and when children began to pray with him, he would pack their things and take them along.

"You shall come to England, too," he told Eva, who stopped crying and just gaped at him in shock. He chose other orphans to join him on the *Kindertransport*, too. One of the school counselors was chosen with us as a chaperone and shepherd. While we children prepared to leave for Prague in a few days, he continued to collect orphans, and I was sent to Nitra to prepare and say goodbye to my family.

We prepared for the voyage at Aunt Giska's house, and she took us all shopping for a brand new wardrobe. Though she was still very reserved, her love was deeply felt and it was hard for me to bid her farewell. I didn't know then that our goodbyes were temporary and that we would spend time together in later years on the other side of the world. When all was ready, and when Dr. Schonfeld was ready to collect us all, my cousins and I boarded the train from Nitra to Prague, where we were going to meet him and all the other children going on the *Kindertransport.*

There were 150 Jewish children, two more than the Home Office allowed him to bring in. All of us had no clue that two of us were being smuggled into England or that there might be potential problems, so we could not worry as we had during the war. We believed, rightly as it turned out, that Solomon Schonfeld would take care of us; that he would take care of everything and that we would be safe.

We were excited and happy. The trip was an adventure. There were six of us in the compartment — Paul and Tommy Krausz, who had been in the orphanage in Nove Mesto with Eva and me, and my cousins Ivan and Anni. Tommy was very good-looking and the object of many a schoolgirl crush, so Eva and I were thrilled to be traveling with him.

The train wound its way out of Prague, lumbering across the ruins of Germany, then through the Low Countries. At every border crossing men in uniform demanded to see our papers and looked through our belongings. We tended to fear anyone in uniform, but there was nothing menacing about these men; they were simply customs officers. The lack of cruelty and hatred seemed to confirm that we were living in a new era, heading for a new kind of life.

At Hoek van Holland on the Netherlands coast, we boarded a ferry that took us across the English Channel, a very choppy ride indeed. It wasn't long before almost everyone aboard was convulsed with seasickness. I was dizzy for a brief moment but never became ill, and I was quite proud of myself for not succumbing—as I saw it—to the misery that had everyone else flat on their backs in their bunks or clinging to the deck rails in desperation. I just took it all in…the salt spray, the gray water, the cold wind pushing us to new shores.

I was not yet eleven years old, but I sensed, as we all did, that we were moving toward better lives. It was 1948, and for the first time since I had been a very little girl the world was at peace. It's what people talked about: peace. How lovely it was; how this wonderful Dr. Schonfeld had promised us wonderful new beginnings. How fine it was that we were all part of it; that we were all together, survivors filled with hope and equipped, though we might not have known it, with our own special resources.

Another chapter was ending, and it was on to the next.

CHAPTER TEN
Arrival in England

Not very long after the sun set on April 22, 1948, the ferry docked in Harwich on England's eastern coast. It was a Thursday night, very dark and cold, with a wet fog that made me shiver. It was just 24 hours before the first Passover Seder was supposed to begin. Dr. Schonfeld, who was strictly Orthodox, was well aware of this, and wanted us all to attend a Seder. He quickly guided us from the wharf to the railroad and put us aboard a train to Liverpool Station, London. Imagine 150 very sleepy children trying to keep their eyes open so they wouldn't miss the slightest thing in this new land. When we arrived in London we practically fell off the train. There we were hustled along platforms and stairs, along walls covered with big posters inscribed with words in a language we didn't understand.

One hundred children who still had a parent, including my cousins, were separated from the rest of us and left for Ireland via train and ferry across the Irish Sea to Clonyn Castle near Devlin, a small village near

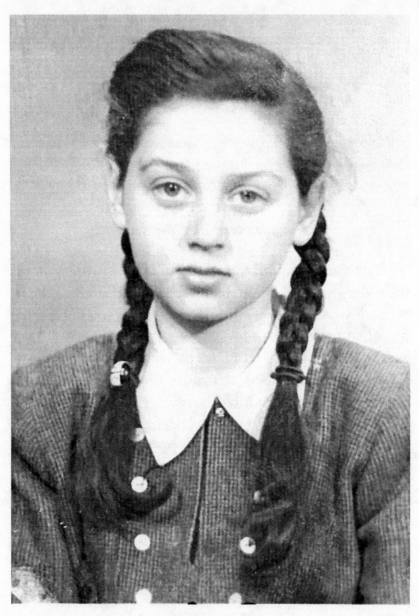

Judith in London.

Dublin. The castle was bought to house these specific refugee children by Rabbi Israel Cohen of Manchester, England. Anni and Ivan were in the group that went to Ireland.

The orphans, on the other hand, stayed in London. Eva and I were among this group. Because Schonfeld had found foster parents for us, we were separated later on and eventually sent off to various households. Initially, however, we boarded a bus and were taken to a house full of cots. We were assigned our sleeping quarters according to age. I took my few belongings, put them under my cot, and then fell into an exhausted sleep. In the morning we were awakened and told to wash and dress. We formed lines for everything and then were fed a breakfast of porridge, bread, butter and a glass of milk. Then doctors gave us physical exams and checked our heads for lice.

For the rest of day we waited and played until we were assigned to the homes where we would be seated at a welcoming Seder table. What I do remember is that I arrived at a home where the people were really welcoming and set a beautiful table that shone and sparkled—reminding me of Mama's Sabbath table and the Sterns' Seder in Budapest. It made me sad, because it brought back bittersweet memories of that time. Unfortunately, I was so exhausted, and then embarrassed, as I almost fell asleep in my chair.

Schonfeld had had his way. None of us missed that first night's Passover celebration, and its significance was not lost on any of us. As young as we were, we understood we were free at last.

England was a very bleak, gray place after the war. It had suffered from the German aerial onslaught, known as the "Blitz." Many streets were damaged and filled with rubble. This gloominess was compounded by London's infamous pea-soup thick fogs, which were insidiously mixed with the coal smoke that spewed from thousands of chimneys until 1952, when strict clean-air legislation was passed. But in 1948, the old-fashioned sulfur-infused smog caused serious health problems and hung like a black cloud over the city.

England was also in mourning. The British had lost hundreds of thousands of soldiers in the war, and thousands of Londoners during the "Blitz." Much of the city center lay in ruins or was being rebuilt. Cranes were everywhere. Rationing was still in effect and there was an air of stringency about the place. Ostentation was out; luxury was nowhere to be found.

The weather was cold and wet; the raw winds from the sea seemed to cut through my frail body. In those days, central heating was rare. Indoor warmth, such as it was, came from the coal fires in fireplaces, the same fires that caused the smog. When you moved away from the immediate vicinity of a fireplace, the air was so cold you could see your breath in front of your face. And because coal, like food, was tightly rationed, it was used in moderation. The solution was to wrap yourself in your warmest clothes, cover yourself with a blanket and wear mittens if you had them. I didn't.

I reacted to the damp cold by getting chilblains. My toes and fingers swelled up and became red and quite painful. The only treatment was to soak your hands and feet in hot water — which didn't stay hot very long in the cold air. The real cure was extended exposure to warmth, and since warmth was hard to come by, I suffered substantially through a bitterly nasty winter.

We orphans were brought to the Stamford Hill section in the northwest of London and settled down in a large mansion rented by Schonfeld. Used as a hostel, it had long hallways and large bedrooms. My room, at the far end of a very long corridor, contained a dozen cots lined up in a very straight row. The toilets and bathrooms were at the other end of that long, narrow, spooky hall. This led to a major problem for me, since I was still haunted by what had happened in the privy so many years earlier.

It was winter and it was cold inside the mansion, especially at night, when the fires were docked. When nature called, it meant I had to get out of a warm bed and walk alone down the cold, dark passageway. The idea terrified me, and so I suffered for a time from bed-wetting.

It horrified me. I was embarrassed, worried that the other children might find out. I was quick to get up each morning and clean up after myself immediately. I would jump out of bed as soon as I was aware of it, and would check to see if there was a puddle under the bed, because the mattresses were so thin. I would sometimes have to grab my towel and clean up the mess and then climb back into the bed and try to find a dry spot so that I could fall back asleep. I was fastidious to a fault and was appalled by my body's response. Between the sense of humiliation and the sense of self-disgust, I suffered — as children with this problem do suffer.

Psychologists today say that bed-wetting in a child who had bladder control problems for a long time is most likely caused by emotional distress. On the surface, I tried to be happy, but you couldn't deny the losses, my illness, and the constant shuffling from place to place. I was one very insecure child — and with good reason. So when I was faced with leaving my warm cozy bed, albeit with my blankets securely wrapped around me, to walk down an endless, scary hallway just to pee, my body made its own decision and I had to wash my sheets daily. Fortunately, Miss Lunzer, the Matron, and all the counselors, nurses and doctors on staff treated me with kindness and sympathy, and I soon overcame the problem.

Maybe it was because they kept us so busy with school that they were able to strip away the nervousness and anxiety we felt when faced with the cultural challenges of living in a new country. I found one ritual, which took place every morning, particularly revolting. As soon as they woke us up to get ready for our school day, before we made our beds, washed up or had our breakfast, we were lined up and fed a spoonful of cod liver oil loaded with vitamins, purportedly to strengthen our bodies. It is as disgusting as it sounds — it tasted like oily, smelly fish, and they gave it to us because it was supposed to prevent rickets, a joint disease caused by vitamin deficiency.

I absolutely hated the stuff. I dreaded each morning, and as my turn came closer and closer, the dread

In school in England. Rabbi Dr. Schonfeld at top;
Judith, top row, second from left.

grew greater and greater. Matron Lunzer had to pry my mouth open to insert the spoon and thrust it past my lips to tip the cod liver oil onto my tongue. That spoonful felt like a jarful, and I would gag. But Matron stood over me and would not go on to the next victim until somehow, summoning all my strength, I would swallow it down. The taste would linger until breakfast, and God help us if we had to burp. It was loathsome. The only stuff that could remove the residual flavor was the porridge they served us. And when we finished breakfast, we walked to school, not too far away. It was a typical English school, and we orphans became part of it.

I attended the Avigdor Primary School on Lordship Road with a handful of my fellow orphans. It was a co-ed school, with more than 200 students from everywhere in London. We all wore uniforms, and went to different classes. The headmistress was the legendary Dr. Judith Grunfeld, who was the spiritual mother and caretaker of Schonfeld's rescued children. At our daily Morning Assembly at the Avigdor School, she would welcome us and then introduce the school's chancellor and founder, Rabbi Dr. Schonfeld.

I remember that at that first assembly he told our story and asked the other students to make us feel at home. We, the refugees, had to quickly adjust to our new surroundings. The next day, we were assigned to our classes and subject to the rules of discipline set forth for us.

And there were many rules. Whenever Rabbi Dr. Schonfeld entered a room, walking tall with dignity, the students rose as one and stood respectfully as he advanced toward the podium of the assembly hall or the teacher's desk. In assembly, we would not be seated again until we sang "God Save the King" to express our thanks to the country that gave us a home, and then *Hatikvah*, the national anthem for the Jewish homeland, the newly-established State of Israel.

Dr. Schonfeld would ask us to sit and then delivered his homily. We would rise again when he called an end to services and left the room—as splendidly and regally, it seemed to me, as the king whose name he bore.

Every day, during assembly, I believed that Schonfeld sought me out among the students in the audience, acknowledging my presence with a tiny nod and a quick smile. This reassured me and made me feel that he was always there looking out for me. At school or at the hostel, whenever I ran into him, he would ask, "How are you, Judith Mannheimer? Is there anything you need?"

I longed to tell him the absolute truth: that I needed my loving parents, my siblings and a comfortable home with my own room and my own bed, where I would feel secure at last. I held back because I was too intimidated and shy to speak so bluntly to such a man. I was happy to be recognized by him, but our encounters always left me speechless. I could only stammer a "no, thank you"—nothing more. Yet the truth is his special attention gave me the feeling that nothing would ever again be as terrible, as lonely or as frightening as my past.

The notion of a special bond between me and the good rabbi was confirmed for me when, out of all the students and *Kindertransportees* he had collected in the British Isles, I was the one chosen to present bouquets to dignitaries attending the Chief Rabbi's Religious Emergency Council (CRREC) fundraiser at the Royal Opera House in Covent Garden. This was a very big occasion and required rehearsal and special privileges—like a new dress and new shoes.

I suffered from a severe case of stage fright before I walked out on the stage, but the excitement soon took over. I stood on the huge stage in that very ornate hall feeling very special when the spotlight shone on me and hundreds of people watched as I made my pretty presentations. But when I looked out at that vast sea of people, all I could see were the silhouettes of their heads!

My studies at Avigdor were my first foray into serious education. I studied French, Latin, Hebrew and English. English was the language of instruction, of course, but none of us was fluent in it as of yet. It was all very foreign and difficult, so I fell back on my formidable ability to memorize material and simply did everything by rote, without understanding what I was saying or doing. The teachers were understanding and kind and, in time, the lessons began to sink in. Math was my favorite subject—it was a language I understood easily. I never had to struggle with it and always felt at home with numbers and mathematical concepts.

I also discovered movies when I lived in Stamford Hill and became a passionate fan. When I wasn't studying, I loved to go to the local cinema and watch gorgeously lush British and American films. Laurence Olivier, Patricia Neal, Vivien Leigh, Clark Gable and Margaret Lockwood were my favorites, and I still love to watch them on cable TV.

Of course, in those days, I was too young to go into the theater by myself. Movies were already rated: 'U' for universally acceptable, 'A' for adults 14 and over, 'X' for adults only. I wanted to see the 'A' movies, so I would stand in line next to some grownups as if I were with them and would give them money and say, "Would you please buy a ticket for me, too." No one ever refused. Together we would enter the theater, then I would thank them politely and go off and sit by myself.

In the dark hall, ensconced in a plush velvet seat, watching the flickering images on the screen, I could transport myself to other dimensions, falling into the stories on the screen. For a few brief hours I lost myself in Shirley Temple movies and films like *Waterloo Bridge*, *The Red Shoes*, *The Best Years of Our Lives* and *Gone With the Wind*. I imagined myself as Scarlett O'Hara or a ballerina in the 19th century. Movies took me to faraway places, acted as my time machine, and taught me about romance. I forgot myself entirely and would be totally immersed in the plots. It was just wonderful. But then, a few hours later, I was back to the spartan reality at Stamford Hill.

Stamford Hill was like a half-way house where we stayed until Dr. Schonfeld found foster homes for all of us, matching families with spare rooms and a need for extra money with children who would fit into their families.

Before we were assigned foster homes, we spent lots of time with volunteer families who invited us to *Shabbat* dinner or to holiday celebrations. Eva's family knew a young couple, the Baders, who lived in Surrey, the green, rolling region not too far from London. They often invited us to spend Sundays with them.

The Baders had two little girls and lived in a charming Tudor cottage with a beautiful garden. Eva and I took the train out on Sunday mornings, rain or shine, always looking forward to our day in the country. Alfred Bader would meet us at the station with his car and drive us to the cottage, where we spent most of the day resting and relaxing. The fresh air, woods, flowers, streams and the family environment were delightful, and I am still grateful for the respite the Baders offered us from the routine in Stamford Hill.

You might think "out of sight, out of mind," and that London was far enough away for my Aunt Giska to forget all about me. But that was not the case at all. She and her family had moved to Vienna after the war, but she continued to keep tabs on her now distant relations. Though my cousins had been sent to Ireland, they soon returned to London. Now Aunt Giska and Yenko regularly sent Ivan and Anni packages with strict instructions to "share everything with Judith."

Unfortunately Anni, who was young and immature, refused to share, while Ivan was more than willing to give me half of the half Anni left him. It was a reminder that family ties, though important, can also be filled with strain, and that siblings can be wildly different from one another. I, in turn, always shared what Ivan gave me with Eva when she was with me.

Eventually, in the winter of 1948-1949, Dr. Schonfeld placed me with a family in Golders Green, a nice neighborhood. (My upkeep at this point was subsidized by Youth Aliyah. After reaching England, my contact with the Sterns was broken forever, and even their "friends" no longer looked for me. I am fairly certain that no funds from the Sterns ever found their way to the CRREC.)

My new "family," the Warhaftigs, lived at 18 Alba Gardens. The husband and wife were educators and had a few children, two of them girls. Helen, my age, and Miriam, her older sister, shared a large bedroom with separate beds and a spacious alcove near the window. They placed a cot in the alcove for me, showed me where I could store my few belongings in a corner cupboard, and, for a time, their home became my home. That small cupboard near my bed quickly became my hiding place where I hid the taffy candies I loved. I had to be so secretive because, among other things, I discovered that the Warhaftigs disapproved of candy.

That winter was a cold one, and I worried about chilblains again. There was not much heat in the house or much warmth in the family itself. They were kind people, but they were very strict and reserved — even more reserved than Aunt Giska! They came to England from Germany long before the war began and had that rigorous sense of discipline one associates with the German character. They lacked a sense of humor or any sense of irony, and they were deeply Orthodox, adhering to every jot of Jewish law and ritual.

We spent lots of time in the kitchen, the warmest room in the house, where we would sit at the table to do our homework or read books. For *Shabbat* they would light the central fireplace in the parlor, where we would spend our time.

As part of my living with them they demanded that I adapt to their ways. I had to say certain prayers, even though I had no idea what I was saying or what the Hebrew words meant. Often I skipped lines just to get it over with. Later, I discovered that among the prayers I had recited were several for men only or prayers reserved for certain holidays—mistakes that would have scandalized them had they known I made them.

The parents also showed me how dogmatic religion could be. They insisted I attend the *Yizkor* (memorial) service held in Rabbi Eli Munk's synagogue (Rabbi Munk was the Chief Rabbi of England) on certain holidays because I was an orphan. I didn't understand any of it. The prayer, in which the dead are recalled by name, is powerful and compelling, and for a young girl it was frightening and forced me to remember what I didn't want to remember.

As the only child told to stay in the sanctuary for the *Yizkor* service, I was marked as different, because other children could go out to play during the service. If they hadn't known it before, after that first Yom Kippur everyone knew I was an orphan with no real home. This deepened my embarrassment about my past and caused me to have trouble making eye contact with the other congregants. To this day I don't think *Yizkor* is appropriate for children, and I am leery of the kind of religious absolutism I saw at my new home. Still, they did their best to make me happy and comfortable.

As a child, the usual procedure on Yom Kippur is to fast for only half a day. When I turned 12, I was supposed to graduate from fasting half a day to fasting the full 24 hours, as would an adult. It began well enough when we came home after *Kol Nidrei*, and I felt fine on Yom Kippur morning. We attended services, but by mid-morning I wasn't feeling well at all. So I returned home by myself and promptly went to my room.

On that Yom Kippur, alone in the house in Alba Gardens, I reached into the cupboard, found my stash of taffy and ate every single one. They were delicious, like forbidden fruit. I felt so much better after the sugar hit my bloodstream that I headed back to the synagogue and joined the others for the rest of the day. But my guilt was so great I couldn't face those grownups. I cast my eyes downward, stared at my shoes and never told them about my secret feast.

For once, life was not such an adventure. Life at Alba Gardens was ordinary, even routine. I had chores to perform around the house, just as the others did, and I didn't feel, as other orphans would later claim, that I was being exploited by the families who cared for us. But I didn't feel comfortable enough there to feel as though I belonged. The atmosphere may have been benevolent, but it was very proper, and in the context of propriety, I was treated as what I was: a foster child whose "parents" were being paid to care for her.

Thankfully, there were grace notes. One was Helen. We liked each other at once. I was a change from Helen's other friends; I think I was a breath of fresh air. Helen was very sweet and smart and, as I responded easily to her interest and affection, we became close. In photos taken at the time we looked as if we were quite the young ladies, with smiles on our faces and our arms around each other's waists.

School was another saving grace. I had moved from Avigdor to the Hasmonean Grammar School, which

At the Hasmonean School.

I loved dearly and couldn't wait to get to each morning. The headmistress, Mrs. Herman, and a teacher named Mrs. Apple, were particularly influential and encouraged me to pursue the subjects I loved: math, arts and crafts, reading, sports and history.

I had many friends and our lives were filled with activity. I can still hear myself calling their names across the schoolyard: Violet! Ruth! Miriam! Vicki! Shoshana! Rivka!

We wore uniforms — dark gray skirts and burgundy blazers with the school badge embroidered on the breast pocket, grey blouses, a burgundy tie, and burgundy sweaters in the winter. I loved the uniforms because they were excellent equalizers — you couldn't tell who was rich or poor, an orphan, a refugee or a native-born Brit; there were no class distinctions based on clothing.

Ruth Corman was an English girl who lived in a beautiful house in Willesden and always invited me to play tennis and go swimming with her. We built an enduring friendship that has lasted to this very day. Ruth remembers me as a thin girl with wavy, medium brown hair. She says I was basically shy, quiet and gentle, until I was crossed — and then I would get angry.

She also claims I was a demon champion at playing dodge ball and that I was so fast that no one could get me out.

Sports built character and physical health, so in addition to our studies we were expected to be very active. My success in sports gave me a great deal of confidence — and a certain "sports hero" cachet around the school. When the school had sports rallies, I would compete in basketball, relay races, the high jump and swimming. Away from the sports field and playgrounds, I carried myself with a serious mien. With my sweater and school necktie, I tried to look decidedly grown-up. I saw myself as a busy, young scholar with a penchant for sports.

I also made a number of other friends when I joined a girls' social group, under the aegis of a local social-service organization. The group, always great fun, met on Saturday afternoons after lunch and offered us the chance to socialize with other Jewish girls and boys while indulging in wholesome activities under the watchful eyes of our chaperones.

The icing on the cake was my bicycle, which I rode to and from school every day. It was a gift from my cousin, Terri and her husband, Emil Hilton. Terri was Aunt Margit's daughter. They'd left Budapest for Australia, and their route took them through London, so they made it a point to see me.

"What do you want most?" Terri asked me when we met at their hotel.

"A bicycle," I answered, immediately and unequi-vocally. And before I knew it, there it was: a classic black Raleigh three-speed "Sports" bike, England's famous "all-steel bicycle." It had a girl's frame (without the crossbar) and had a basket attached to the handlebars for my books. That bicycle was a great joy and gave me the freedom and mobility I never had before. It gave me the opportunity to explore new places simply by hopping on and pedaling as far as my legs could take me—and I sometimes had to remember that I had to have the energy to pedal all the way back to Golders Green.

Helen had a bike, too, and we cycled to school together. The distance from Alba Gardens to the school on Holders Hill Road was about a mile and three quarters, not much of a trip. But we did have to cross the formidable intersection at Finchley Lane and Great North Way to get there. I was always ready for the challenge, sitting upright on my splendid black charger, in my burgundy and gray uniform, with my books safely stashed in the basket on my handlebars. I was certain that I looked like a real English schoolgirl—and I felt like one, too, as I led Helen across the wide expanse of black asphalt as vehicles swerved to avoid us.

In 1949, I discovered the power of books. The most potent escapes of all were achieved without moving any major muscle groups at all; all I had to do was crack open the covers of a book. Looking back, I realize that most of my time in Golders Green that winter was spent lying under the covers in my cozy bed reading novels. There was a second-hand bookshop nearby, and the bulk of my pocket money went into its coffers. I read Jane Austen and the Brontes, Dostoyevsky, Tolstoy, and every book in the *Little Women* series by Louisa May Alcott. I loved period romances and Gothic adventures. I would read and read and read, and then I would daydream about possibilities and fantasies that had never occurred to me before.

I traveled in fact as well as in fancy. During the summer holidays I spent time in Cardiff, Wales, on the River Taff, a seaport with a sizeable Jewish population. The port was always busy, and the surrounding seacoast offered wide expanses of sandy beach. For a girl who had never seen the sea until I crossed the English Channel, the beaches were an interesting and beautiful distraction.

A young Cardiff couple with a baby took me in as a mother's helper in exchange for their hospitality. Eva was nearby at the Pinnick home. They fell in love with her, with her beautiful big black eyes and sweet character, and instantly adopted her. The following summer, I went back to visit her in her "new" home and we were just two carefree kids lolling on the beach, occasionally braving the chilly surf and playing in the sand.

The students from the Hasmonean School were also brought to Bournemouth, a seaside resort, where we spent a month just having fun. Boys and girls lived in separate dormitories, though all the sports and activities were co-ed, and we had a marvelous time.

During one summer break, one of my dreams was fulfilled, and I was sent to a ballet school north of London, where I had a brilliant time. I was with a company of girls my age who adored ballet and together we followed the career of the inimitable Margot Fonteyn, ballerina par excellence.

Rabbi Dr. Schonfeld was a constant presence in my life. As chancellor of both schools, he was  always on site, walking the halls, popping his head into one class or another, watching us at our games. He always had a pat on the shoulder for me, always asked how I was doing, always acknowledged my presence and was attentive to what I said. I was sure he was following my progress in school and at the Warhaftigs, keeping track of my growth and well-being. It gave me a sense of self-confidence I sorely needed. He was a savior sent at just the right time to save me from total despair. He saved my life and my Judaism.

This was an extraordinary gift, and it is one for which I will always be grateful. I tried to tell this to him when I was living in Israel, in the 1950s, and called on him. Nothing had changed. Rabbi Dr. Schonfeld smiled broadly, fixed his warm blue eyes on mine, and asked "How are you, Judith Mannheimer? Tell me about your life now."

Many years later, after my marriage, I saw him by happenstance on a street in London. "Dr. Schonfeld," I said, "It's good to see you."

He looked at me in that intent way, and I was certain he did not recognize me; after all, he had known me when I was a little girl and I was now a mother. I shouldn't have been surprised that he knew me at once. "It's Judith Mannheimer, isn't it?" he said.

In 1982, I represented children from the *Kindertransports* who lived in the United States and Canada at a testimonial dinner in London honoring Dr. Schonfeld on his 70th birthday. Irwin came with me. My responsibility was to present him with a book written by the now-grown children he had saved and educated. The event was held in a huge auditorium filled with thousands of people. For Irwin this was a whole new introduction to Dr, Schonfeld's accomplishments. Though he was already very ill, Dr. Schonfeld was there when the master of ceremonies announced that "Judith Mannheimer Alter Kallman" would make a special presentation to the man who'd saved thousands.

The auditorium was packed with *Kindertransportees*, many with their children and grandchildren in tow. And there on the stage sat the one man largely responsible for their existence. The thousands upon thousands of people born of the remnant saved by the *Kindertransports* represented a victory. It was true that millions had perished, but those who survived, like the thousands of young and old gathered in the auditorium that night, were rebuilding the Jewish people all over the world.

On that night I was reunited, for the first time since 1950, with my best friend Eva Steiner (who had since married a man named Freilich). When Eva heard my name announced from the stage, it jolted her into action. She roamed up and down the aisles, stopping at every row, searching faces of the women, looking for me.

Finally she thought she'd found a familiar face and stared at me. "Judith?" she asked, hesitantly, making sure she was right.

I am ashamed to admit that I did not immediately recognize her, not having seen her in decades. My best friend had been a young girl, and now the woman standing before me was a middle-aged, very Orthodox matron. Her head-covering also altered the shape of her face. Since I wasn't expecting to see her in London, I drew a blank.

"Don't you recognize me?" she asked.

I shook my head.

"It's Eva Steiner," she said, and began to cry.

So did I. The years fell away, and I thought about how we'd met at the sanatorium in the Tatras; how we had been sent to Nove Mesto, and how we came to be rescued by Dr. Schonfeld. The memories of the suffering that had preceded our friendship and the extraordinary changes in our lives since then flooded our minds.

We wrapped our arms around each other and could not let go.

"It's a miracle," Eva insisted, "a miracle." It was the end of February, and Purim was not far off; miracles were on people's minds. "Judith is my angel," Eva explained to my husband Irwin, "she took care of me."

The next day Eva came to my hotel with a *Megillat Esther*, a parchment scroll of the Book of Esther, which details how the Jewish people were miraculously saved from genocide in Persia.

"It's a miracle our meeting again," she said. "It's like the miracle of Esther saving the Jews all over again," and pressed the *Megillah* (the Book of Esther) into my hands. We stayed in touch from that day on. Years later, Eva sent me an astonishing wedding invitation. Her child was marrying Paul Krausz's child—it was *that* Paul, Paul from the train—who'd come with us to London so many years ago. For years people wondered what had happened to him, and now destiny was showing her fine hand.

I never had the chance to present the book to Dr. Schonfeld that night. His strength failed him as the gala evening wore on, and he was forced to leave early. I gave the book instead to a committee member who passed it along. I hope he had a chance to read it before he died in 1984. I hope he knew how grateful we were to him for deeply touching our lives in so many important ways. For me, and for so many of us, he appeared at a crucial moment and provided us with the tools we needed to build our futures.

I am also grateful to the British government for giving me refuge, security and freedom, all very precious commodities. The years I spent in England were important, formative years and caused me to gain much-needed maturity. I received formal schooling that was freely given and through wise exposure learned about new ideas, new places and new people. In England, for the first time in my memory, I lived a normal life, a life made up of school and friends, sports and movies, bike rides, summers at the beach, a growing interest in dance, art and fashion—the opening up of new possibilities.

Though England never offered me the loving warmth I had known in the bosom of my family in Pieštany or at the Sterns in Budapest, it was in England where my life was graced by mentors like Dr. Schonfeld, Dr. Judith Grunfeld, Mrs. Herman, Mrs. Apple and by lots of loving friends who opened their homes to me. To me, England will always be what Shakespeare called it—"this precious stone set in the silver sea"—a rare jewel I will always cherish.

CHAPTER ELEVEN
Journey to Israel

By 1950, I was chafing under the strict discipline and dogmatic religious requirements of living with my foster family. Leaving Alba Gardens each morning to go to school was a relief. I was restless. I missed my siblings, and I wanted desperately to reconnect with them. As luck would have it, they lived and worked not far from each other in central Israel: Turi and Bubi were in the Israeli Defense Forces and Bella worked in a Bezalel factory that made souvenirs for tourists.

I had plenty of help making my decision to move to Israel. In addition to providing us with appropriate teenage fun and experiences, Ezra, a local youth organization, held social gatherings on Saturday afternoons that fueled our idealism and our Zionism. Over time, as we talked and listened and argued, we became aware of our responsibilities as Jewish youths in the post-war world. We were inspired to think about immigrating to Israel. Idealistic Zionism mixed itself into my desire to reunite with my siblings, and that proved to be a potent combination. I was sure Israel would provide me with the secure family home I still sought, and my caretakers were willing to make it happen.

Arrangements for my departure were made through Youth Aliyah, and in the winter of 1950 I boarded a train at Victoria Station and headed to Marseille, the oldest city in France and the busiest port on the Mediterranean.

Marseille was different from any place I had ever been. Ancient limestone wharves dominated the city's waterfront, reflecting the bright, white Mediterranean light into the brilliant turquoise sky. The colorful international melting pot/open air market atmosphere was startling and exotic. The Youth Aliyah dormitory was in a very old fortress-like building and housed children from all over Europe. I was shocked to find that the dormitory bathrooms were co-ed! I was a proper English schoolgirl, after all, and this was my first encounter with the French, whom I found very exotic indeed.

I stayed in Marseille for a couple of weeks while Youth Aliyah found accommodations for me aboard any ship that was headed to Haifa. I used that time to improve my French by chatting with merchants, for I had rudely discovered that learning a language in a classroom was decidedly different from trying to speak it with the locals.

A few weeks later, I found myself onboard a ship, but I am not sure if I was on a legitimate passenger vessel or a freighter that took passengers. The trip did give me a few more days to practice my French with the crew, who wore wonderful white uniforms and looked like movie stars. Of course, I fell madly in love with all of them. They were very kind and gave me the grand tour, which included a trip to the bridge to see the wheelhouse and meet the captain.

I spent as much of the voyage as I could on deck, and was still a good sailor, even when we hit rough seas near Stromboli, off the foot of Italy's boot. Being on deck was infinitely better than staying in our sleeping quarters. Our berths were near the engine room and smelled of gasoline, and our bunk beds were tightly stacked one on top of the other. It wasn't the most pleasant experience, but after the boring routine of London, the voyage — the ship, the good-looking sailors, the swell of the sea — put adventure back in my life.

The journey was also a rite of passage, for it was aboard ship that I first began to menstruate, and this both frightened and embarrassed me. I was only remotely aware of the facts of life — sex and reproduction were rarely discussed in those days, especially in a household as tightly wound as that of the Warhaftigs — and it was never discussed at school.

Since I had no mother figure to talk to me about such things, I was ill-equipped and emotionally unprepared to deal with this abrupt onset of womanhood. I went into shock, but I was also resourceful, so I told no one and improvised a solution. I could not even bring myself to share the news with my sister when I arrived in Haifa in December 1950 or January 1951.

Asher/Turii, Bella, Judith and Moshe/Bubi.

The greatest joy that came from landing in Haifa was the reunion with Bella, Moshe and Asher. It surprised me to see how grown up and good looking they were. At first, they seemed almost strangers to me and I had to reconnect with them. I discovered that my brothers had Hebrew names now. Bella was still Bella, but Bubi was called Moshe and Turi was Asher. Bella was beautiful and had thick, lustrous black hair that fell in waves to her shoulders. She had a tall, gorgeous figure, and her looks reminded me of our mother. Bubi had grown into a very handsome man. With his dark hair and fine features he reminded me of Gregory Peck. Turi, too, was handsome, with wonderful thick hair. But where Bubi was narrow and lithe, Turi had an impressively athletic body. I was proud to be part of that family, for we made a handsome foursome.

All the children on the ship, including me, were sent to a Displaced Persons' camp on Mount Carmel, where we stayed until Youth Aliyah found places for us around the country. While we waited, the Israelis taught us modern Hebrew, which was more difficult to learn than I imagined it would be.

I was placed in Kfar Batya in Ra'anana, about 12 miles north of Tel Aviv. I was very lucky, for Kfar Batya was a model children's village funded and operated by the Mizrachi Women of America (now AMIT). Turi/ Asher had been an early resident of the village, soon after he'd arrived from his Displaced Persons Camp in Cyprus.

Mizrachi is a worldwide movement for religious Zionism. Founded in 1902 in Vilna, Lithuania, its motto is "The Jewish people in the Land of Israel living according to the Torah of Israel." The women's division was founded in 1925 by Bessie Gotsfeld, a New York housewife who envisioned an organization that would control its own funds and operate its own projects in pre-independence Israel. The organization's primary focus was religious Zionist education, and it began taking in children from Youth Aliyah less than a year after Hitler came to power.

Kfar Batya — officially known as the Bessie Gotsfeld Children's Village and Farm School (Batya is Bessie's Hebrew name) — was the organization's first children's village. It was founded in 1947, and its mission, to this day, is to absorb and educate immigrant children and troubled Israeli youth.

Kfar Batya.

All three of my siblings were delighted with my placement at Kfar Batya, which was considered a great prize. But there was a downside. We weren't able to spend much time with each other because visiting hours at the children's village were limited, and so was my siblings' free time. And though it wasn't far from Tel Aviv, Kfar Batya wasn't easy to get to. For Bella, who lived in a women's hostel in Jaffa just south of Tel Aviv, a trip that was essentially a straight line between two points was a frustrating journey on two buses that took the long way around. The trip was doubly difficult for my brothers because they could visit me only when they were on military leave. Still, though we never lived under the same roof again, the surviving Mannheimers were, at long last, together, and it felt wonderful.

Kfar Batya was sprawled across vast acres of rolling fields and hills. Israelis and American visitors alike came to tour its facilities, gawk at its modern architecture, and marvel at the fact that there was never a speck of litter to be found on the grounds.

A long dirt road led like a spine from the main gates straight to the fields in the distance. Paths branching off of it led to dormitories and school buildings. As you entered the gates, to the left there was an office complex/infirmary, where I worked after class, and the dining hall, a large building with glass walls that that were usually kept open in the Mediterranean climate.

Lush gardens separated the office from the dining hall, which was our social hall and acted as an energy-radiating central meeting place. The greenhouse was behind these two main buildings, and beyond that, up a hill, were the bright white villas that housed the counselors, faculty, and some of the older children.

On the right side of the spine were four large two-story dormitories of stark white stucco with red tiled roofs in traditional Mediterranean-style. To the right of the dorms, there was a large vocational and academic school building.

Surrounding the compound, in every direction, were the fields where children, who had perhaps never in their lives lifted a hoe, learned to farm — and did so well enough to make Kfar Batya self-sufficient and able to feed all its inhabitants. The village was home to 150 transient students who ranged in age from 6 to their late teens and was the permanent residence of the administrative, teaching and maintenance staffs. Although primarily an agricultural school, they also taught weaving, shoemaking, sewing, carpentry, locksmithing, tool making and landscaping. Every student was given work assignments.

We rose at six a.m. Before breakfast, our first work assignment was to clean the cottages or dorms in which we lived — unless we were on kitchen duty. In that case, we had to race over to the dining hall to get breakfast ready for the entire village. Everyone, from the youngest child to the oldest staffer, would march in at the appointed hour, all of them dressed in shorts and open-necked shirts. We sat at long tables that had vases that were always filled with flowers from the greenhouses. We blessed the food we grew ourselves and then noisily and happily consumed it. After breakfast, there were classes or work assignments. Schedules depended on work assignments, which changed each week.

When I arrived at Kfar Batya, I was given a bunk in one of the dormitories and assigned to food service. That meant working in the kitchen and dining room, doing whatever needed to be done, from food preparation to waitressing. Later, I was assigned to the greenhouses, where I worked with the flowers and plants. After a few months, I moved into a cottage I shared with four other girls and was assigned to work in the infirmary, next door to the village's administrative offices.

I loved working in the infirmary, where real doctors and nurses gave me a deep sense of responsibility. I took temperatures, gave out aspirin, and made sick children comfortable. I felt important when I carried out the doctors' instructions, and I was treated as an important person, which helped me develop my self-esteem.

My main assignment, earned by default, was to act as a public relations ambassador whenever English-speaking guests came to call. My superiors had me welcome them. I served them refreshments and was instructed to show them the grounds. Many of these visitors were philanthropists who wanted to see their money hard at work in our innovative educational venture.

I enjoyed practicing my English on our guests, and I was aware that by doing my job well and pleasing people, I was fulfilling my assignment.

Mr. Chaim Zvi Enoch was in charge of the children's village. I don't know his background, but I will wager it was military because he ran the place like an army general. He demanded discipline and cleanliness and was tough with children who did not live up to his standards. His idea of applying discipline was to twist the miscreant's ear and swing the child around until he or she was weeping in pain—and to do so in front of whoever was around, thus adding insult to injury.

Rigorous as Enoch's discipline was, it was probably necessary. Kfar Batya was filled with orphans from all over the world. Many had survived by their wits on the streets of Europe and Northern Africa—mean, tough streets that in wartime reeked of depravity and crime. Enoch knew how to handle troublemakers and

Judith on a tractor.

maintain control. The iron fist with which he ruled kept everyone in the children's village safe, even if we did not warm to his personality. On the other hand, if he liked you, you could do no wrong in his eyes; he never punished his favorites.

I steered clear of Enoch as best I could, but my ability to speak English brought me to his attention—and made me a favorite. There were only a few counselors who had any proficiency in English, and fluency in the language was a plus in the American-financed village. The assumption was that my English meant I was better educated, more cultured, and, I suppose, more worthy of his attention. In any event, his favoritism meant that I was unofficially but absolutely exempt from agricultural work assignments, so while I sometimes rode the tractor with other kids, it was for fun and not because I had to work in the fields.

Enoch's favoritism resulted in another important honor for me, although at the time I was unaware of just how great a brush with history it was. In 1951 a very important visitor came to Kfar Batya from America and caused a flurry of intense activity around the compound. The excitement built day by day as we made everything gleam and shine—dormitories, classrooms, animal barns—nothing was left unscrubbed. There wasn't a weed in the flowerbeds or an errant shirt flap protruding from any child's shorts. I felt the excitement of that "visiting day" quite personally, as I was chosen to help the youngest child present flowers to a great lady.

The grand personage we prepared for was Eleanor Roosevelt, the former First Lady of the United States of

America and, at the time, I had no idea who she was, only that she was important. Yet her looks surprised me. She was, to a young person like me, a very old lady—ungainly, unpretty, unfashionable, with bucked teeth and a squeaky voice. Still, there was something about her. When she smiled, her face seemed to light up from within, and that's when her real beauty was evident to everyone around her. When she asked us to talk about our lives, I felt her sincere interest and concern, an authenticity that endeared her to millions.

Not everything went as well as I had hoped. At night I dreamed my parents were looking for me and would find me. Of course, it was only a dream, an ephemeral chance to escape from reality, as fanciful as another fiction I carried in my head, namely that one of the Americans I guided around the village would instantly love me and want to adopt me and whisk me off to America to join a ready-made family that would embrace me warmly.

But orphaned children have to learn to accept reality and as I grew older, I felt my losses more and more. The certainty that I was missing something vital in life, something that could never be retrieved, deepened the void inside me, which seemed to grow larger and blacker and emptier with time.

The care and attention we received from counselors and teachers helped relieve my despair. So did the pattern of the days at Kfar Batya, which brought a reassuring stability to our lives. They kept us so busy — so tightly scheduled—that we had no time to release the emotions that lay just below the surface.

One day, I gave the guided tour to two couples and a single woman, all from the United States. One of the couples was very friendly and when the tour was over they hung back and asked me about myself. When I mentioned I had been in the last *Kindertransport* arranged by Rabbi Dr. Schonfeld, the man I was talking too was clearly startled. "Solomon Schonfeld?" he asked. I nodded.

"I am Moses Schonfeld," he said, "and this is my wife, Ruth. Solomon Schonfeld is my brother."

Moses Schonfeld was a New York-based journalist with the United Nations, and he couldn't get over the amaz-

Judith and Moses Schonfeld.

ing coincidence. Here, before his very eyes, was a child his brother had brought to safety. It created a special bond between us, and for months after he and his wife had returned to New York I received packages from them that were filled with lots of goodies and other luxuries for an orphaned schoolgirl.

I was permanently assigned to the infirmary, and I didn't have to work in the kitchen or clean up the dining room anymore. I still tended to my own cottage and indulged my passion for cleanliness in the infirmary, which I regarded as "my place," a place I kept absolutely spotless. This earned me points with "General" Enoch.

The dean of academic programs and my principal at Kfar Batya was Rabbi Dr. David Eliach. He is a wonderful educator and teacher whose standards have always been rigorous and whose expectations were high. He favored students who excelled in their studies, and I had a hard time meeting his standards. Needless to say, I was not one of his favorite students. Modern Hebrew was difficult for me.

Eliach was especially impressed by one brilliant student, Yaffa Sonensohn Ben-Semesh. She was a Holocaust survivor like me, and she became an important Jewish scholar. When Yaffa graduated, he married her and they moved to America where he established himself at the Yeshiva of Flatbush. (Years later, my daughter Debbie became one of his excellent students.)

Since there were no academic records to which to refer, at Kfar Batya they placed their students in age-appropriate classes for history, literature and religious studies, all conducted entirely in Hebrew. It was a lot to ask of me, so I concentrated on the subjects I liked — math and art — where it didn't matter if I was fluent in Hebrew or not.

Despite my less than stellar academic record, I was thriving, busy with work. I was attractive, tall, and carried myself with the confidence that came with being an accountable and responsible person.

But I wasn't stuck up or stuffy and was surrounded by good friends. Sometimes I grabbed the chance to take piano lessons from an American woman who lived in Ra'anana and had three daughters of her own. Whenever I took the bus to my lessons at her home, she greeted me with milk and cookies.

Edith Gross was my very best friend in Kfar Batya. Her family had emigrated from Hungary and lived close by in Kfar Shmaryahu, then just farmland near the seashore. They paid partial tuition so that Edith could get an education.

Edith Gross with Judith.

Unfortunately for them, Edith hated Kfar Batya. I don't know if it was because of "General" Enoch's military discipline, the work assignments, or the rhythm of our lives in the children's village, but Edith could never adjust. One day, Enoch reprimanded her — not with the hard fist of punishment, but with a tap of reproach — and that did it. Edith told me she was going to run away, and planned it for a Saturday morning, when there was less supervision and the fields were empty. Edith lit out across Kfar Batya's fields, heading west toward the sea and home.

I hadn't spoken to her or seen her before she took off, but I guessed she was heading to Kfar Shmaryahu. When I could not find her, I decided to go after her, running through fields that smelled of dust and sun and that were alive with the droning of insects. Sure enough, I found her, lying on her stomach in the tall grass, sobbing into her arms. She was the picture of misery. I begged her to come back. I told her things would be even worse if she didn't, because leaving the village without permission was a serious violation of the honor code. I was worried about the consequences for her—and for me—if she left Kfar Batya. She was, after all, my closest friend.

Edith, stubborn as she was, was bound for home and her loving parents. (It seemed to me that I subconsciously chose as my friends children who had parents and conventional homes.) There was no way to convince Edith to go back to the village. I thought it over, decided to forget the consequences and go with my friend. I absolutely could not let her go off by herself. So I left, too—also without permission—but with my friend. We walked through fields thick with wheat, and others that were freshly plowed and raked. We could see footprints and tractor tracks in the dirt, until we finally came to a dirt road, which led us to Edith's parents.

It took about three very hot hours to arrive, sweaty and thirsty, at the Gross's apartment. Her parents were shocked to see us. But they were happy we were in one piece. They served us a good lunch and insisted that we go back.

They convinced Edith that returning to school was the best thing to do. I was greatly relieved, but it meant that Edith and I took another three-hour hike, arriving back in Kfar Batya late in the afternoon. I don't think anyone discovered our disappearance because we were never punished. I was happy. I had my friend Edith at my side, and things were good, at least for a while. Edith had her own demons and really wanted to get away from Kfar Batya. At the end of the semester, she went to live with her parents and later married at age 17. Perhaps that was her escape from whatever was haunting her.

CHAPTER TWELVE
Life in Tel Aviv

Kfar Batya served children through elementary school, and by 1952 it was time for me to move on. I wanted to continue my studies, but I craved the city life. I applied to a girls-only academic/vocational high school with room and board in Tel Aviv, the one Israeli city that was a magnet for the sophisticated, the place where everything trendy and cool was happening. I was thrilled when I was accepted at Beit Zeirot Mizrachi-Tel Aviv, which offered courses in business administration and home economics. It was located smack in the center of the city. I arrived in August 1952 and loved everything about the school, the city, the proximity to my siblings and the life; it was all vibrant and inspiring.

The school was founded in 1938 and was another showpiece for the Mizrachi Women of America. The school, the dorms, the administration and Mizrachi offices were in a beautiful three-story building lined with balconies. The high school on the second floor was dominated by a long, cool hallway with high ceilings and stone floors, with airy, bright classrooms lining both sides of the hall. We, the students, lived on the third floor and had a dorm mother, Mrs. Davis, who was strict to a fault but still very kind. She kept the place well organized and spotless.

The Mizrachi office suite on the first floor was an interesting place to me because it was filled with an ever-changing group of delightful American women who had volunteered to come to Tel Aviv. They worked for months at a stretch to help raise funds and do whatever it took to fulfill the Mizrachi mission, before they returned to the States where they spread their success stories to all who would listen. I was friendly with many of them, which gave me the chance to practice my English.

I wanted to be sophisticated intellectually, so I took courses in philosophy, literature, advanced math and science. Classes and work assignments alternated between mornings and afternoons. We were assigned as *sous-chefs* in the huge kitchen, and as busboys and wait staff in the even larger dining room. We cleaned the dorm rooms, or served as gatekeepers, which required us to keep track of everyone who came and went. Occasionally I cooked, waited tables, and cleaned up after dinners held for visiting Mizrachi VIPs. I requested this work because it allowed me to earn some money.

I also continued to act as guide and Mizrachi spokesperson to potential donors and VIPs. These show-and-tell tours allowed me to improve my English and provided me with access to English language books, which I loved. I chose gymnastics as my physical education program and was often in one of the top rungs of the human pyramids we built. My favorite extra-curricular activity was drama club, and I adored every moment — performing in comedies, melodramas, and tragedies. It didn't matter what I did, I just loved the costumes and make-up that allowed me to act out new experiences in the safe world of make-believe.

Even so, I often worried that I would forget my lines and ruin the play. Stage fright would grip me until I stepped into the spotlight, then it would miraculously disappear. I developed enough confidence from these experiences to gain poise and grace — enough of it to consider modeling as a career.

I loved dressing well, and thanks to Mama, style was in my genes. By then I was 5 feet, 6-and-a-half inches tall, weighed 105 to 110 pounds, had an 18-inch waistline and was very fashion-aware. When I window-shopped on Dizengoff Street, where the boutiques were, shopkeepers asked if I had time to do some modeling. I was flattered by the idea that I was pretty enough to be asked. Though I wasn't paid initially, by the time I was a senior I regularly modeled for a prominent commercial photographer, who sometimes did indeed pay me. It was mostly a good

Judith and Bella.

experience and brought me closer to the business side of fashion and fashion design.

The school also sent us out on field trips to learn firsthand about Israel. Teachers, guides and chaperones accompanied entire classes and smaller groups as

On a school field trip.

we toured the country from north to south and east to west. It wasn't such a big place, we discovered. We studied Jewish history on site, watching it come alive as we stood in the places whose names we'd read in the Bible. These trips touched the depths of my heart and soul. Sometimes we held relics of that history in our hands. We visited brand new cities, ancient tombs, prehistoric hills, and the wells of sweet water that kept our ancestors alive for millennia. We traveled from Lake Kinneret to Jerusalem, from Ein Gedi to Tsfat (Safed) to Beersheva on spiritual, historical and amazing journeys into the past of our people.

Living in Tel Aviv also made it easier for me to see my brothers more often and to visit with Bella, who shared an apartment in the very old and artistic town of Jaffa, directly south of us on the Mediterranean coast. In those days it was very poor and primitive. Though she'd suffered terribly after the deportations and had a difficult passage to Israel in 1948, she had become

Asher/Turi.

Moshe/Bubi.

a vivacious, fun-loving woman. Despite the lack of formal education, Bella was well read in many subjects and highly cultured. She was particularly interested in music and absolutely passionate about opera. She constantly dragged me to concerts and operas so she wouldn't have to go alone. At first I hated it, but I grew to appreciate what I saw and heard, and years later, dragged my own children to such cultural events — with similar reactions and similar results.

Bella lived in a women's hostel, where space was limited. When people were away for the weekend, Bella would invite me for a visit since only then was there a bed available to sleep in. She mothered me. She loved to see me in nice clothes and often spent her hard-earned money on items she thought I would like or needed. She was kind and loving and just what a big sister should be. We always had a good time together, and hanging out with her and her friends made me feel very grown-up. True, we didn't always see eye to eye on things, but I still treasure the memories of those days. (Eventually Bella married and moved to Australia, and Bubi married and moved to Canada. Turi stayed in Israel, married and raised his family there.)

There were also, gratefully, four Mannheimer cousins and their families scattered around Israel for us to connect to in Tiberias, on Kibbutz Nir David in the Jordan Valley, and in Jerusalem.

They were a generation — or perhaps half a generation — older than I was and mothered me, too. My cousin Miriam and I became close friends — I would visit her family in Jerusalem and do interesting things.

Baba Schwartz and her son, Riki, my old friends from 10 Rombach Street, were also in Tel Aviv. Baba came to Israel with her sister and her son Yossi on whom I had a crush. We visited with them often and it was like visiting relatives; Baba was like an aunt, and I always considered Riki as a brother. Alas, he was infatuated with me and insisted we would eventually marry. His passion was wasted and his heart broken since I refused, in any manner, shape or form to think of him romantically—but I was still very flattered.

Bubi/Moshe often visited me at school and sometimes took me to dances. After all, taking your sister to a dance was a safe way to meet girls, and going to a dance with your older brother was a great way to meet boys. In those days, our social lives were positively puritanical compared to today's dating scene. Sex before marriage was unheard of for

Beit Zeirot, Tel Aviv.

"nice" Jewish boys and girls, especially for nice religious Jewish girls from Beit Zeirot Mizrachi. When we went out, it was boys and girls in a group. As a group we took hikes in the mountains, danced at folk festivals and went to the movies. House parties were "in" and they were fun, but not like the wild house parties kids have today. We'd all arrive together and be served non-alcoholic drinks and snacks. We'd spin vinyl records on the old Victrola and dance the night away. Foxtrot, tango, rumba—I was crazy about it all—I was a typical teenager, ready to go anywhere, try anything—within my own strict limits—and meet anyone I hadn't met before. I had an appetite for life, and at Beit Zeirot in Tel Aviv I was *alive*.

When I graduated, I went to work as a bookkeeper at the Union Bank in Tel Aviv. I lived at Beit Zeirot a while longer and still played tourist guide to visiting VIPs. One of those assignments was a blessing in my own life. I was honored to be assigned to Bessie Gotsfeld, beloved founder of Kfar Batya, who was by then in her late 60s and quite frail. She gave me many insights into life and comforted me with warmth and wisdom.

I took her for walks, read to her, and shopped for her. It was a great way to get to know this legendary woman, and caring for her also brought me into contact with the presidium of Mizrachi Women, which was a rewarding experience for me. While I stayed at Beit Zeirot, I got my regular salary from the Union Bank, enjoyed an active social life in the city, and went on excursions around Israel. I even had a boyfriend or two. Riki persistently discussed marriage, but it was hopeless. As good-looking as he was, I was unable to see him as anything but a brother, the little kid I had known on Rombach Street. Thankfully he moved on and in due course married Leah, one of my classmates.

As my 18th birthday approached, so did the need to make a major decision. Every Israeli citizen is required to enlist in Army service at 18. I was exempt because I was still "institutionalized" at Beit Zeirot, which was considered a religious facility. I knew if I were ever to leave Beit Zeirot I would never commit to an Orthodox life, so my only options were to enlist or marry.

I wasn't opposed to serving in the army but, at the time, I wasn't willing to commit two years of my life to it. Much of my life had already been taken from me and I rebelled at the idea of two more years of being told what to do with every minute of my life. That left me with the option of getting married, something I intended to do one day, but not just yet. I still wanted to go to university, and that did not seem compatible with marriage. I would also need to meet someone worth marrying, and that hadn't happened yet, either. Anyway, for me life was still too full of adventures and fun to consider making serious commitments to a man and to children.

One morning in July, I was assigned to Howard Alter, a visitor from America staying at the Dan Hotel. The next day, when I called the office for information, they said Mr. Alter was standing right in front of them and was asking for me. They put me on the phone with him, and he told me he had a gift for me from Lee Stein, one of the Mizrachi women from America. He then asked if we could meet for dinner. We dined the next night at the fancy restaurant on the beach in the Dan Hotel. He ordered beef tongue for both of us and I was appalled. I let him have my dish, and he announced: "They say if you eat your date's meal, it means the two of you will marry." I was unmoved. He was a serious-looking man, much older than I, with a hairline that was just beginning to recede. Yet he had a wonderful dry wit and great intelligence. And there was something very comforting about him, an easygoing manner that put me at ease at once.

Howard had never been to Israel before and was obviously excited about visiting the new nation. He was there to visit his 75-year-old grandmother in Jerusalem and was on a mission to learn about Mizrachi's work in Israel. Howard was also vice president of the National Council of Young Israel.

So when he asked me to show him around, I was more than willing to do so. For the next few days I gave him my standard tour of Beit Zeirot and the main attractions in Tel Aviv. He was exceptionally nice, but from the beginning it was clear that he was smitten with me while I was not smitten with him.

Howard was easy to be with; the awkwardness all came from me. As time passed, our age difference came to have less meaning for me and I was willing to be seen with him in public. I was learning to communicate with him and we spent lots of time together, right until he had to return to the States, with a stopover in Paris.

From the City of Lights he sent me a pair of exquisite sunglasses and a beautiful letter. He wrote simply and eloquently that meeting me was the best thing that had ever happened to him, and he hoped we could correspond.

We did. Every other day or so, throughout the rest of the summer and deep into fall, I received letters from Howard and answered them. They were wonderful letters, all about America, his life there, his work, his family and his interests. We got to know each other really well. The most beautiful letter of all arrived in November, and it was something of a shock: Howard proposed marriage and said he wanted me to leave immediately for the States so I could meet his family. My fantasy in Kfar Batya had come true!

Bella was the first to hear my news and joyfully urged me to go ahead. Out of respect for her—she was the oldest, after all—I wondered if it was appropriate for me to marry before she did. But she dismissed that out of hand. Generously and graciously, she wanted what was best for me and believed this marriage was right for me. "Marry Howard," she urged. "He's a good man, and it's a good opportunity."

Howard was offering me love in a new world, with a new life and new possibilities. It would give me a chance to be more than a bank clerk and offered the security, the family and home I always craved. I decided I would do it: I would go to America, meet Howard's family and marry him.

I accepted his proposal, sealed the letter, applied the stamp and dropped it in the nearest mailbox. By the time I woke up the next morning I had changed my mind. Panicked, terrified, I sent Howard a telegram telling him to disregard the letter he would eventually get, because I could not marry a man who was many years older than me and who I didn't know very well. I wasn't even sure I liked or loved him. This dramatic pronouncement did not deter Howard. He wired back saying that he refused my refusal and was on his way back to Israel to see me.

I was flummoxed by his reply, perplexed, confused, uncertain what to do or how to act. So I told the Mizrachi women who had "adopted" me (Natalie Resnikoff, Dvorah Rabinowitz, Belle Goldstein, Ella Lewis and Mollie Golub) and asked them what they thought I should do. After all, they were brilliant and were in charge of the organization. "Should I marry this man?" I asked.

To a woman, the Mizrachi establishment was outraged, even stupefied, and their reaction stunned me. I wrote to Howard and told him what they said. It upset me to have to tell him their "opinion" of him, and I worried about his reply. But I needn't have. Howard was unruffled. "Just tell Mollie Golub this," he wrote, "just tell her I'm a son of the Alter family."

I did and Mollie's jaw fell to the ground. Then her mouth curved into a huge smile. "You're the luckiest girl in the world!" she crowed, "They are the nicest family in the world." The others agreed. This sudden and overwhelming approval of the entire group clinched the deal. Everything was wonderful, and we made plans for my visit to the States and our marriage. Howard arrived in Tel Aviv in December, with a return ticket for him and another one for me.

Howard and Judith on their wedding day.

No wedding is easy, and neither was this one. Since I hadn't served in the army, the Israeli government would not let me leave on a tourist visa. Their policy placed military obligation first, a vacation in America second. Howard suggested we tell the government we were engaged to be married; we'd obtain the appropriate papers—falsely—and fly off to the States. It seemed a good solution, but Bessie Gotsfeld wouldn't hear of it, and Bessie was a formidable naysayer.

In her eyes, I was one of hers—a Kfar Batya girl, a Beit Zeirot girl, a child of Mizrachi Women of America. False papers were out of the question. "You will get married here," said Bessie. "I will give you the wedding, and it will be at Kfar Batya."

And it was. We had only a few days to arrange the reception, and after Bessie alerted the Kfar Batya staff,

Howard, Bessie Gotsfeld and Judith.

they got to work as only they could. The timing was lousy all around. Howard had just opened a business in New York City and was feeling pressure to take care of it. His parents and two brothers were unable to come to Israel for the wedding because of previous commitments. That was a great disappointment. Nevertheless, his grandmother in Jerusalem joined us for the ceremony and celebration.

Everyone at Kfar Batya, students and staff alike, cooked and baked. Kfar Batya flowers decorated the marriage canopy and the great dining hall. The Kfar Batya musicians played. And Howard paid for it with a generous donation to Mizrachi Women of America.

Bella and I went to the boutique where I used to model dresses. We ordered a custom wedding gown—a beautiful white and silver brocade—and a complete trousseau, as well as Bella's maid of honor dress. Howard paid for everything, and also bought me a white fur bolero to wear over my dress if it got chilly. And because I was afraid of being taller than my husband-to-be, I wore flats.

The *chuppah*, made from a prayer shawl, was set up outside the social hall on December 28, 1955, a cool, bright, late afternoon. I am told I was a beautiful bride. I walked down to the ceremony with Bessie Gotsfeld on one side, and Howard's grandmother, Bracha Goldfarb, on the other. Howard was waiting for me under the *chuppah*, and I remember how handsome he looked in a dark suit with a flower in his lapel.

We honeymooned in Herzliya, traveled to the Galil (Galilee) and stayed in Tiberias for a few days while we waited for my American entry permit. Of course, being Israel, it took longer than expected. But Howard's uncle, Sid Alter, a State Supreme Court judge in Brooklyn, had a connection to Herbert Lehman, the U.S. Senator from New York. Between the judge and the senator, my immigration paperwork was expedited.

In January 1956, we boarded a flight to Vienna, Austria to see my Aunt Giska and my cousins, who showered us with gifts and gave us the grand tour of the city. And then we flew on to Switzerland to see my cousins there before we headed to New York City.

It was like living a dream.

Chapter Thirteen
A Family of My Own

I finally said goodbye to Europe, boarded a plane and flew into New York on a chilly winter's day. Howard's parents, Sadie and Morris Alter, were at the airport to greet us. They immediately treated me like their daughter and devoted themselves to making me feel at home. They introduced me to everyone they knew, and made my first few weeks in America a mad whirl of parties.

Howard had two brothers. Aaron was in medical school in Chicago, and Jerry and his wife Estelle lived in Far Rockaway, not too far away. We became close. The first time I visited, Estelle took me by the hand, opened her closet, and said: "Take what you want." Her openness and generosity were irresistible, and she became my first friend in America.

Aunt Giska's daughter Barbara and her family lived in Annapolis, Maryland. They came to visit shortly after I arrived, and Barbara took me shopping for clothes. My cousins from Toronto, Zoli and Kati Warly, came to New York to meet us as well. Zoli's mother was my father's sister, Rozsi, and like the Ungars, they were considerably older than I was. Barbara's children were my contemporaries, and I spent my time with them whenever I went to Annapolis.

Rabbi Solomon Goldfarb, my husband's uncle from Long Beach, Long Island, also came to meet me. We talked and when he heard my British accent he wanted to know more about me. Howard told him that I was one of Rabbi Solomon Schonfeld's famous *Kindertransportees*, one that had arrived in London on the last shipment of children from Europe.

Uncle Sol looked shocked and proceeded to tell us a story of his own. He had invited a guest speaker to his congregation, a journalist with the UN, who told his audience the dramatic story of a young girl who once gave him a guided tour of Kfar Batya and who happened to have been on the last *Kindertransport* organized by his brother.

The rabbi told the journalist that the story sounded familiar. He wasn't sure, but he'd heard that his new niece was also on that *Kindertransport*. And when Moses Schonfeld asked him who that was, he was surprised to hear that it was a certain "Judith Mannheimer."

Howard, a CPA by training, worked long hours to nurture the Howard Notions and Trimming Company. He'd learned the trade years earlier by working for his father in a shop on Manhattan's Lower East Side. But ever ambitious, Howard wanted a place of his own and thus opened a wholesale notions and trimmings house on Grand Street. Bedeviled by the issues that plagued many new startups, he developed a pattern of working long hours that persisted throughout our marriage. Nevertheless, before long, I became his assistant bookkeeper.

As I became more American, I signed up for a design course at the Fashion Institute of Technology (FIT) in Manhattan. I also took a class in spoken English, to see if I could rid myself of my British accent because I wanted to sound like an American, too. Howard and I would drive into the city together every morning. I would head to my classes, and when I was done, I would go to the store and do the books.

I looked and felt like a schoolgirl. I was still a teenager—right down to my saddle shoes and bobby sox—so young and innocent as I commuted between the two sites by subway. But by this time, I was a pregnant schoolgirl, and it was my pregnancy that spurred us to find our own place, an apartment close to Jerry and Estelle in Far Rockaway.

L ife was good. I was busy, happy, and warmly embraced by an extended family. Most of all, I was married to an exceptional man, who had a sense of humor that, like the finest champagne, was dry like *brut*. Every day I fell more and more in love with him. He had a good mind and knew many things I found fascinating. People jokingly called him "Alter Winchell" because, like the notorious columnist for New York's *Daily Mirror* and *Newsweek*, Howard had an answer for everything.

I continued working and studying up until I felt my first contractions. We were watching *War and Peace* in a movie theater when the pains began. We immediately rushed straight from the theater to Maimonides Medical Center in Brooklyn, where Aaron, Howard's brother, was an intern.

The agony was worth it, for when it was over I had the most precious gift of my life, the daughter I always dreamed about. Deborah Renée was named for my mother and my sister. She was the Alters' first granddaughter, and she was the first posthumous grandchild of my parents.

Motherhood had been a fantasy to me, but the reality was very different than I had imagined. I had had so little experience being a daughter that I never realized how deep the love is between mother and child. Debbie was my living doll. I could not let go of her, could never get enough of her. I played with her constantly and read to her all the time. I loved to dress her up, and was always sewing little outfits for her. I was utterly ecstatic. Here I was, in America, married to a wonderful man, and the mother of a beautiful daughter.

I still attended classes at FIT but did the bookkeeping at home. I became friendly with other young mothers in the neighborhood who discussed diaper services, pacifiers and Dr. Spock. I learned to play bridge and Canasta. Life fell into a happy and fulfilling routine.

This lovely routine continued, punctuated by two more pregnancies and the births of my beloved sons. Jonathan David was named for my father, Jonah. (Jonathan was also the name of my maternal grandfather; David was my paternal uncle.) Robert Shlomo was named for my brother. One of his Hebrew names is Baruch, the male equivalent of Bracha, Howard's grandmother in Jerusalem, who died not long after we were wed. She was, in a sense, one of the reasons we married and deserved to have one of our children named for her. As a little boy, Robert, who was born on the Fourth of July, always thought the annual fireworks were set off in his honor. I never really disabused him of the notion and told him he was my special contribution to America.

Before long we bought a big, comfortable house in Far Rockaway, and in it we lived a wonderfully blessed life. Zionism was just as important as Judaism to us. We visited Israel often, and the trips always stirred my soul. In my life of enforced wandering, Israel was the first place that had given me a sense of belonging. Its land, its people, its very air, allowed me to connect to my sense of self. Bringing my children "home" to Israel was a chance to wrap them in my own spiritual identity.

Israel was also a burgeoning, modern country that was learning how to turn deserts green, feed a population explosion and cope with the ever growing need for water. Howard was deeply involved with Ampal, the American Israel Corporation, that been had putting seed money into Israeli companies since 1942. His work gave him access to, among others, Israeli

Judith with Israeli Prime Minister David Ben-Gurion.

Judith with Israeli Prime Minister Golda Meir.

Judith with Israeli Prime Minister Menachem Begin at
President Chaim Herzog's nephew, Isaac Herzog's, bar mitzvah,

prime ministers David Ben-Gurion and Golda Meir and Jerusalem's most famous mayor, Teddy Kollek. Of course, he would take me along and introduce me. In the wildest fantasies of my youth, I never, ever could have imagined that one day I would be chatting with Israeli prime ministers and Jewish leaders!

Then everything ground to a halt as we waited with bated breath for the outcome of the Six-Day War in June 1967. When Israel won, we were buoyed by her victory! We felt so proud.

I took care when it came to telling my children about my past. I never concealed it, and I never talked about it with anger. Rather, as each of my children reached the age I had been when my losses began, I simply told the tale of my childhood. I tried to make the telling as natural as it would be for any mother drawing a comparison between her children's era and her own.

When I spoke of my parents, it was to tell my children what I remembered of what they were like. I did not say how they died, because I did not know and because the point of the story was the life of my children's grandparents, aunt and uncle, not their deaths. My aim was to help my children deal with these events in a way that would not frighten them or cause them pain. By turning those events into stories from long ago, they became part of the fabric of our family life.

There seemed little connection between the girl from Piešťany and the suburban housewife with her bridge games and volunteer work on Long Island.

Indeed, there was only a minimal amount of Europe left in me; only a trace of my origins was evident in who I now was. I sought out American-born friends and wanted to stay away from immigrants who came to America after the war. I didn't need reminders, I didn't want to talk about it, I wanted to get on with my oh-so-American life.

And then the bottom fell out. While we were visiting family in the summer of 1971, Aaron, then Chief of Hematology at Maimonides, noticed a dark swelling on the side of Howard's leg, just below his knee.

Howard had dismissed it.

"Get it checked out," was Aaron's advice.

Howard went for tests and discovered that he had a malignant melanoma and that they needed to operate immediately. We held our breath, prayed and hoped. And for a while, it seemed everything would be okay.

Autumn turned to winter. Life was sweeter than ever, now that we had put the cancer behind us. On December 25, 1971, we celebrated Jonathan's bar mitzvah. In the summer of 1972, Howard had a relapse and after a bitter struggle, passed away on December 15, 1972.

There was a great void again in my soul. I was in shock, my world shattered. I felt as if I had lost a limb, a part of myself. But I knew I could not fall apart just yet. I had to represent strength to my children and stretched every fiber of my being to rise to that challenge.

I was a young widow and had two major tasks. One was carrying on Howard's business. Work saved my life, though I always insisted on being home when the children returned from school. Work also provided our primary income. The Howard Notions and Trimming Company enabled me to provide my children with an excellent education and to raise them in freedom and comfort.

I needed to make my children feel that we were all in this together, that they were part of everything that was going on. I shared my thoughts and feelings with them. I wanted the children to air their own feelings,

(l-r) Jonathan, Debbie and Robert.

and make them feel the security I never felt as a child.

Was it painful? At first, it was very painful indeed. After dinner every Friday, we would sit in the family room, telling each other what our week had been like. It didn't matter what we talked about; anyone could comment at any time. The kids would talk about school, their friends, or maybe things that were bothering them, and I would discuss the business, the house, and family events. If one of us had a problem, we would all explore possible solutions. If the discussion ended, we would just sit together—maybe talking, maybe reading, just being together.

Those Friday night sessions became, as I had intended they should, the adhesive that linked us together. In due course, when the kids invited friends for dinner or to spend the night, they were welcomed as part of our family. This closeness was essential to our emotional stability.

CHAPTER FOURTEEN
My Children Grow Up and So Do I

Robert's bar mitzvah took place eighteen months after Howard's death. Afterward, people continually advised me to start dating again. It was an utterly foreign notion to me. I hadn't had a real date since I met Howard, and that was decades earlier.

I wasn't even interested in going out. My spare time was reserved for my children, and that was that. I began taking the kids to Grossinger's in the Catskill Mountains for the holidays and it turned into an annual family tradition, giving us a chance to meet new people we liked and who liked us. We were constantly invited to family lifecycle events around the world, bar mitzvahs and weddings in Australia, Switzerland, England and Austria. These changes of scenery were always enjoyable.

But going out to meet new men was not something I could get used to. It took a while for me to agree to enter the dating game. I had married young and when I went out as a girl, it was always with a group until I married. So, at first, I didn't feel comfortable.

Only when I realized how lonely my life had become, and when I missed and needed the recognition and encouragement that a loving partner could provide, did I start dating again. Dating as an adult is not much different from dating as a teenager. Nor does marriage, widowhood or motherhood confer any particular wisdom where matters of the heart are concerned. In the beginning, in fact, I felt like a 16-year-old—immature, uncertain, a bit awkward. I suffered the anxieties of the lovesick, waiting and wondering if a man I liked would call back, and I invented excuses and stratagems that bordered on the ingenious in my attempts to elude a man I wanted to avoid. It took me eight and-a-half years to find someone to care about.

I didn't know what I was looking for, although plenty of friends were willing to offer their opinions on the subject. Despite their input, I knew I was attracted to intelligence, kindness, character, a good sense of

(l-r) Robert, Judith, Debbie and Jonathan.

humor, and, of course, "chemistry." While it's often easy to find two or three of these attributes in a single individual, it's not so easy to find all of them. Sometimes two or three qualities are enough, and sometimes, even one can blind you to the absence of others. Some of the men were wonderful and some were duds. Sometimes I knew from the very outset that no relationship was possible.

At one point, I decided marriage was not for me. I was going to enjoy life as it came, and wouldn't worry about male companionship; even though I continued dating, my attitude had changed. Some friends advised me to "dress down" when I met a man for the first time; not to wear my red fox coat or drive to the meeting in my Cadillac Seville. "You'll frighten the guy," friends told me.

"If it frightens him," I replied, "he's not for me."

It was like being told to "act dumb" so you won't intimidate a date—as if I could even conceive of a relationship with someone threatened by my intelligence! I was not about to apologize for my achievements or intellect. I had gone out and done something for my children and myself, and I was proud of that. In the meantime, the children flourished,

making their way through school and on to college.

While they lived at home, I shared my life with my children and they shared theirs with me. In fact, our house seemed to be a magnet for young people, as my children's friends from school and the neighborhood descended on us like birds coming to a favorite roost.

I met Irwin Kallman by mistake because of a social faux pas committed by a mutual friend. My friend and Irwin were both dining, separately, at a restaurant on City Island, a historic seaport community near the Bronx. When he spied Irwin at a table across the room, he assumed that the young woman Irwin was with was his daughter. It was, however, his date! To atone for his error, our friend decided to make a *shidduch* (a match) between me and Irwin as "penance" for embarrassing him.

Irwin duly called and we made a date for lunch. He was smitten, and a few months later I decided ours was a relationship worth developing. Irwin was kind, generous and a delight to be with. By March of that year, Irwin and I were seeing quite a lot of one another. And in April, when the children and I went to Grossinger's in the Catskills for Passover, I missed Irwin so much that I packed up some of the resort's famed pickled herring and lox and drove more than 100 miles to his apartment in New York. They say the way to a man's heart is through his stomach, and the pickled herring seemed to do the trick. That spring, we traveled together to Portugal and Spain—a wonderful trip—and when we returned, we realized that we didn't want to be separated again.

Irwin, a lawyer, is a born and bred New Yorker; a graduate of the famous Stuyvesant High School and City College. He did a stint at the University of Michigan to see if he wanted to be an urban planner, but preferred business and attended New York University, receiving his MBA in 1951. He then went on to New York Law School. A tax attorney, he specialized in real estate investments, and then formed his own company, Win Properties. When I met him, he had been divorced for ten years and was the father of two grown children, Patricia and Jonathan.

What struck me at once about Irwin—what strikes all who meet him—is his brilliance and his sense of humor. From the beginning, he made me laugh—with his storehouse of great stories that are wonderfully delivered with razor-sharp wit and profound wisdom. And the chemistry between us developed to perfection.

Of course, there were miscommunications, mostly due to my imperfect grasp of American idiom and customs. Irwin lived a far more secular life than I, and I had no ear for the rhythms of mainstream American life. Early in our courtship, over dinner one evening, he said: "If you play your cards right, we can go far together." I had no idea what he was talking about, so

Judith and Irwin on their
wedding day.

when I got home I called a friend to find out "What is this card game I have to learn?"

Another time, Irwin invited me to his home in Harrison. When I arrived, I was dimly aware of soft music playing in the background and noticed that Irwin lit votive candles that looked like the *yahrzeit* candles lit in Jewish homes on the anniversary of a death. It was the weirdest thing I had ever seen. So I asked him, "Who are all these memorial candles for?"

He broke into unrestrained laughter and said, "So much for trying to be a romantic!"

And I started laughing, too, which was much more romantic than the candles.

By the summer of 1980 we were "going steady." Then, in January 1981, Robert, who was about to enter dental school in California, went to see Irwin and put it to him plainly. "If you and my mother are planning to marry," he told Irwin, "here are the dates I'm available. Pick one."

Irwin picked June 3, 1981. And that's when we were married in his house in Harrison. In attendance were our children and a few close friends. We honeymooned in Paris and on the Riviera, came home and threw a big reception for ourselves at the Mamaroneck Beach & Yacht Club. It was simply splendid.

Eighteen months after we were married, Debbie, who lived in California, gave birth to my first grandchild. It was the most joyous news possible.

Though Irwin and I were now happily ensconced in our marriage, I remained open to adventure and

Our families, joined forever, at our wedding.

opportunities. One day a friend of mine called. She was working on a movie called *Six Degrees of Separation* and wanted to know if I would be willing to be an extra in the film. I said, "Sure." Before I knew it, I was doing the tango with a stranger and dancing the night away at the elegant Rainbow Room, high atop Rockefeller Center in Manhattan. I even got the chance to meet actor Will Smith, and since the scene did not land on the cutting room floor, I guess you can say I'm a star, too.

I also expanded my interest in the arts and began to study sculpture. The results of those endeavors are on display in my garden, and they continue to inspire me in following my artistic inclinations.

Irwin and I have had more grandchildren since that day — and years of happiness in being together. Ours is a wonderful marriage. From heart to heart, from mind to mind, we are with each other. We love to travel, to entertain, to socialize, and have a terrific time doing things together. Irwin has long been involved in various political causes and we've been privileged to meet many dignitaries, like Prime Ministers Benjamin Netanyahu and Menachem Begin. We visited with President Bill Clinton and his First Lady (now Secretary of State) Hillary Rodham Clinton at the White House and have participated fully in American political life.

My husband and my family are the most important things in my life. We inherited each other's children when we married and blended two families. Our children love each other and we love all of them equally.

It is a blessing for me to be able to share my love for him with them and all the grandchildren and great-grandchildren; they care for him as much I do.

Mine is a good life, blessed in many ways.

Judith with Prime Minister Benjamin Netanyahu.

Judith with First Lady Hillary Clinton.

The Kallmans with President Bill Clinton and Vice President Al Gore.

Judith with Israeli President Chaim Herzog.

Debbie, Simon Wiesenthal, Judith and Irwin.

Judith with Vice President Walter Mondale.

New York's Senator Chuck Schumer with Judith.

Judith with Senator Joseph Lieberman.

Irwin, Hillary Clinton, Judith and NYC Mayor Rudy Giuliani.

Judith with Robert F. Kennedy, Jr.

CHAPTER FIFTEEN
The Unexpected Detour

"Hope, like the gleaming taper's light…"
– Sir Oliver Goldsmith, *The Captivity. Act ii.*

Irwin and I were in Geneva, Switzerland at the beginning of September 2001, at the beautiful Richemond Hotel, one of the city's oldest and most elegant hostelries. The dining room was very Old World and filled with beautiful people. The dinner was delicious and the company convivial.

I became aware of a woman across the room who stared at me as if she knew me. She was a striking woman, stunningly attractive and dining alone. I thought she looked familiar as well, so as we rose from dinner I stopped at her table.

"Do I look familiar to you?" I asked her, in English.

"Are you American?" she asked.

When I nodded, she invited me to have coffee. Irwin and I joined her.

She introduced herself and proceeded to tell us her astonishing story. She was born in Russia and moved to Italy when she was still very young. She claimed she had been mistress to a series of powerful political figures, most of them from the Middle East. In due course, she married the head of security in Libya, one of the Ghadafis. She claimed she had "lots to tell the American and Israeli security services." She needed an American contact to help her find asylum and special protection.

She was living full-time in the luxurious and elegant Richemond Hotel, where the Middle Eastern clientele was treated with kid gloves. She was suing her husband for support for herself and her daughter, and was seeking a new home, preferably in the United States. She offered a simple trade: information for political asylum.

And what did she want from me? I was to be the messenger who would get her message to the right people "because," she told me, "I know the dangerous things that are going to happen in America."

"What can happen and how do you know?" I asked.

She proceeded to describe how America was going to be subjected to major terrorist attacks, to suicide bombings and more. She'd gone to the American embassy in Geneva and asked to see the head of the CIA, but they wouldn't allow her to see him. She then sought him out at another location and gave him her information, but she was dismissed as an eccentric. The same thing happened when she approached security officials in Israel, also seeking asylum. Though she feared for her life and that of her daughter, she would not give over her information until she received a guarantee of safe haven.

It seemed to me to be a preposterous story, something out of a second-rate spy novel: innocent American tourist meets mysterious European with a shady, Mata Hari-like past. Yet I believed her. So I gave my word that when Irwin and I returned to the States on September 11, I would do what I could. She gave me her card and a packet of faxes and news clippings about herself. We said goodnight.

When I saw her at breakfast on the morning of 9/11, I went to say goodbye.

"You're returning to New York today?" she asked.

And suddenly I was fearful. If what she had told me was even half-true, she used information as a weapon. All at once it dawned on me that the less information she had about me, the more secure I would feel. I shook my head. "Actually," I lied, "we're going to London today. We'll return to New York later."

"All right," she replied, "but don't forget, I need your help."

Irwin and I boarded our Swissair flight for New York later that morning. We were in first class, and I settled in with my book. I would occasionally glance up at the movie screen to track our progress on the map. I loved to watch the progress of time and mileage and looked up now and again from my book to see how far we'd come and where we were in our path across Europe and out over the ocean.

Three hours into the flight, I looked up at the screen and was astonished by what I saw. The plane was flying back across its own contrail; it had turned around in mid-air. I didn't know if it was a problem with the projection or if something was really wrong. I tried to wave down a flight attendant to ask, but the flight attendants were racing toward the cockpit, heedless of me and the other passengers. Panic spread through me. Then two flight attendants appeared at the front of the first class cabin and asked for our attention.

"Ladies and gentlemen," one began, "there has been a tragedy." I froze. I assumed there was a bomb on the plane and that Irwin and I would die. I was wrong, of course. I was stunned by what came next. "New York and Washington have been attacked," he said. "The World Trade Center and the Pentagon have been bombed. It is estimated that 50,000 people are dead. We have been ordered to return to Geneva."

I became hysterical. Our children were in New York, so were my grandchildren, my friends, my home, my life. I could not believe—could never have imagined—that the United States, bastion of democratic strength and unrivaled military might, could be touched by anything or anyone. I could not believe that enemies could have pierced the protective shield America had built around herself. I believed that in America I was secure from every danger. Such an attack simply could never happen there. I knew it was war, that the misery of my childhood was starting all over again, that there would be the kind of destruction I thought I had escaped forever.

I reached for the air-to-land phone and tried to call each of our children in New York, but it was impossible to get through. Then it occurred to me that I could call Debbie in California. And for a moment, I got through. "Debbie!" I cried out. "Debbie! Debbie!"

Then the connection went dead. As I sobbed uncontrollably, the feelings of fear so common in my childhood began to surface. The flight attendants grew alarmed. They brought me soothing drinks, talked me "down," and stayed with me until I grew calm.

We went back to Geneva. Swissair personnel attended to our every need and tried to make us comfortable. We returned to the hotel, where we were glued to CNN and the phone. As I learned that everyone I knew was safe, I regained control of myself. Our mysterious acquaintance was at the hotel.

"I thought you went to London," she said.

"No," I admitted. "We headed for New York, and then this happened."

She said to me: "This is what I'm talking about, and it's only the beginning. But no one wants to listen to me. Do something when you get back to the States. Please."

American air space was shut down for days. No planes, except military jets and flights that took members of the bin Laden family back to Saudi Arabia, flew in or out of the country. We waited it out in Geneva, where we were comforted by the synagogue services on Friday night and by spending time with my relatives. As always, community and ritual brought some solace.

A few days later, Irwin and I finally were able to return to New York and, in time, our lives resumed a normal routine. But my sense of unease was unabated.

I presented our acquaintance's "case" to Henry Rosenberg of AIPAC, the America-Israel Public Affairs Committee, but nothing came of it. I then told her story to guests at a dinner party and one of the guests, a New York State Supreme Court judge, the Honorable Sam Fredman, said, "This cannot ride," and asked the Federal Bureau of Investigation (FBI) to get in touch with me.

Subsequently, Irwin and I went on a short trip. When we got back, I found a message from the FBI asking me to get in touch with them. I gave them my story and faxed them the papers that had been given to me, along with the woman's business card. I never heard anything about this matter again, not from the FBI or anyone else. I often wonder what happened once they got that material, especially since they were under scrutiny for failure to communicate with other intelligence groups like the Central Intelligence Agency.

Whether the mysterious lady's story was true, partly true or a total fabrication I do not know. I know I believed her far-fetched story and that the timing of her warning, so close to the events of September 11, awakened fears long dormant. If Washington and New York are vulnerable, I realized we are all vulnerable.

There was more. The September 11 attack was inextricably tied to hatred for Israel and the Jewish people. In its wake there was evidence of a rising tide of global antisemitism. I had seen this before. I knew what it could do. I had been its victim. And now it seemed to be happening again.

After 9/11, all the old terrors came rushing back to me. The sense of loss, the bitter memories, the fear of the unknown and the unexpected, all came to the fore. I was bereft. But Irwin assured me that all was not lost. He would take care of me; we had much more living to do, and would be very happy.

Irwin was right; we have much to look forward to. I am watching my grandchildren and great-grandchildren grow up. There are new sights and sounds, fresh adventures, movies, plays, music, dance and art to experience, to raise our spirits and mend our souls. And there is the house in which we can grow old together.

God is with me; He has been with me always, from the lost world of Piešťany to 21st century America, across continents and oceans, in times of fear and perfect confidence, through calamity and unutterable loss and in every moment of golden happiness. My faith in God's presence is absolute. It is as much a part of me as my flesh and blood; it burns within me.

As I look back on all that I've been through, I know my miraculous survival happened for a reason. I had to bear witness to my past, to speak for my parents and lost brother and sister. When others read of their stories, they become part of the collective memory and soul of our people and the people of the world. My children and their children have already enriched our society—they are wonderful and productive and work to make the world a better place. I hope that readers have heard my voice and will learn something from these pages; to make better choices, to act when necessary, and to understand that we are all alike and that we all have goals and dreams.

The candle in my heart is one of hope, and its flame is eternal.

EPILOGUE

I began with a story about one of my granddaughters; I end with a story about my oldest grandson, Evan Goldenberg. Evan's bar mitzvah in November 2000 was the first family bar mitzvah at the Western Wall in Jerusalem. It was a difficult and dangerous time. The Intifada had begun several weeks earlier and tourists stayed away. Our entourage—the immediate family, a number of Debbie's and Mark's friends from Los Angeles, Mark's parents—were an anomaly in the tourist-free streets of the City of Gold.

It was a difficult time for me as well. Irwin could not join us because he was ill and I was loathe to leave him. Nevertheless, I took a flight out on a Wednesday night and returned to Irwin that Saturday night.

Evan's bar mitzvah ceremony was held at daybreak on a rooftop adjacent to the Western Wall. As the sun rose and poured through the graceful archways over the ancient walls and gates of the city, it turned the stones their famous golden hue. "Ten measures of beauty were bestowed upon the world; nine were taken by Jerusalem and one by the rest of the world," says the Talmud.

Those words resonated with me that day, as I was filled with a sense of belonging to Jerusalem. I had never been so aware of the City of David or more connected to the Jewish people who for two millennia had read the prophecies of Isaiah and Jeremiah, yearned for the Temple, a return to the homeland and the complete restoration of its capital.

I stood surrounded by my children and grand-children, listening to my oldest grandson's voice chanting the ancient prayers, the words rising up over that holy place. The spirit of Israel and its people flowed in my veins, like an electric charge that reinvigorated my soul.

It was one of the most spiritual moments of my life. I finally understood the oneness of everything around me: the holy city, my family, the roots from which we all spring, the future standing before me in the form of my grandson as he recited words that were rooted in the past.

Later, we marched to the huge plaza in front of the Western Wall, the last remnant of the Holy Temple, with Evan bearing the Torah in his arms under a protective canopy like a groom embracing his bride at a Jewish wedding. We danced until I thought I might collapse with joy. When Debbie and Mark dedicated the Torah scroll in honor of Evan's grandparents and in memory of his great-grandparents, Jonah and Dora Mannheimer, I understood I was witnessing a miracle.

The heritage of my parents was alive in Evan, who was embracing the Torah, and it was alive in all of my grandchildren. Since then, Kyle, Kevin and Austin have had their *bnai mitzvah* in Israel. My two granddaughters, Alexa and Samantha, have celebrated their *batei mitzvah* in Israel as well. I have succeeded in passing on the legacy. The candle in my heart was the spark that lit the way for others to follow. The light of the Sabbath candles from Piešťany now burns in the hearts of my children, my grandchildren and great-grandchildren. They will be true to their heritage, and this book, I hope, will allow that commitment to glow forever in the hearts of generations still to come.

OUR FAMILY ALBUM

HaGaon Reb Chaim Tzvi
Mannheimer, my father's
great-uncle, a reknowned
Torah scholar.

My paternal great-grandmother, Fani Bernfeld Mannheimer.

My paternal grandfather, Moshe Mordechai Mannheimer.

My paternal grandmother, Fani Leah Fischer Mannheimer.

Gaon Rav Anshel Neumann, my
maternal great-grandfather.

My maternal grandmother,
Ethel Neumann Ungar.

My maternal grandfather,
Jonash Ungar.

My mother with her older sister Margit.

My mother (r.) and a friend.

My mother (l.) and her sister, Margit.

Barbara and Dave Ungar (Giska's daughter and her husband).

My mother's three brothers and their wives.

The Katscher family.

The siblings in Budapest, 1942.

With Bela in Budapest.

Judith in her military-like unifrm.

Judith in Kfar Batya (bottom row, third from left).

Class picture: Judith in Beth Zeirot in Tel Aviv
(top row, fifth from left).

On an outing in the Galil
(Judith, far right).

Judith at work at the Union Bank.

Bella at work in Israel.

Bubi/Moshe in Israel.

Asher/Turi in Israel.

With Bella in Israel.

Bubi/Moshe, Judith and Asher/Turi in the 1990s
at the Western Wall in Jerusalem.

Great-grandson Jack and Judith.

Great-grandson Sam and Judith.

Family photo.

A Candle in the Heart — 289

In Memoriam

Pieštany Memorial.

לזכר עולם

יהיו חקוקים פה אשתך הצדקת

מרת אסתר בת רחל

ובנה אשר אנשל ושני בנותי

ובתה דבורה ובנה ובתה

וחתנה יונה

וכלתה יטל בת חיי שרה

ונכדה הבח'יעקב כ"ץ

שנהרגו כולם עקהלש באישוויטץ

ובשאר מקומות בשנת תש"ד-וה

תנצבה ה'י'ד

Ungar family memorial.

Jonash Ungar's headstone.

Ungar Family Tree

Rabbi Akiva Ungar (1813-1881) == ??
     |
Moshe (Moritz) Ungar (1843-1916) == Nettie (Eszter) Abelesz (1843-?)

Israel Abelesz (18??) == Leni (18??)
     |

| Jonash (1869-1943) | Izrael (1870-?) | Mari (1873-?) | Iczig Wolf (1874-1894) | Jakab (1876-1881) |

Rabbi Anschel (Adolf) Neumann (1809-1881) == Devorah Schmidl

Abraham Naftali Schmidl == ??

Moshes Shmuel Neumann (d. 1911) == Rachel

Jonash Ungar (1869-1943) == Etelka (1869-1944)

- Margit = Jeno Katz ✡ (1895-?)
  - ┌ Tibor ✡
  - ├ Terri = Emil Hilton—Andrew - Michelle
  - ├ Ella = Tibor Wagner—Tom
  - └ Erwin = Judy
- Alador = Louisa (1896-?)— Arthur = ? ┌ Bettina
  - └ son?
  - Kurt = Terry
    - |
    - Evelyn = Michael Gross
  - ┌ Sharon = Alan Vidor - 4
  - ├ David
  - ├ Nicky = Zoltan Waldman - 4
  - └ Michelle = Andrew Silverberg - 3
- Armin (1897-✡) = Irene ✡ — Anita ✡ & Claire ✡)
- Izzy (1902- ?)
- Dora (Dvora) (1904 - 1942) ✡ (see page 301)

✡ died in the Holocaust

Mannheimer Family Tree

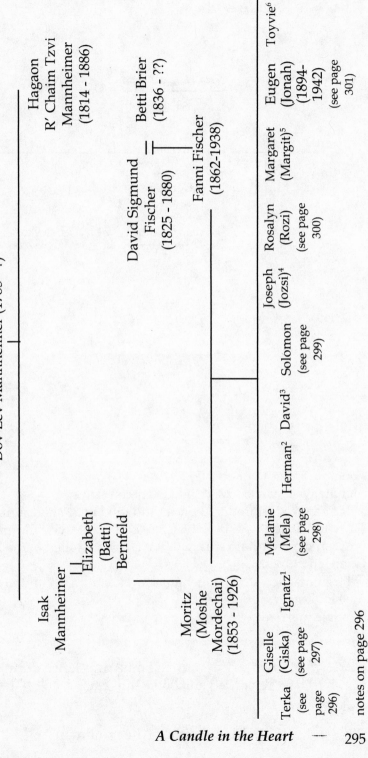

Dov Lev Mannheimer (1785 - ?)

Isak Mannheimer

Elizabeth (Batti) Bernfeld

Hagaon R' Chaim Tzvi Mannheimer (1814 - 1886)

Betti Brier (1836 - ??)

David Sigmund Fischer (1825 - 1880)

Fanni Fischer (1862-1938)

Moritz (Moshe Mordechai) (1853 - 1926)

Terka (see page 296)

Giselle (Giska) (see page 297)

Ignatz[1]

Melanie (Mela) (see page 298)

Herman[2]

David[3]

Solomon (see page 299)

Joseph (Jozsi)[4]

Rosalyn (Rozi) (see page 300)

Margaret (Margit)[5]

Eugen (Jonah) (1894-1942)

Toyvie[6] (see page 301)

notes on page 296

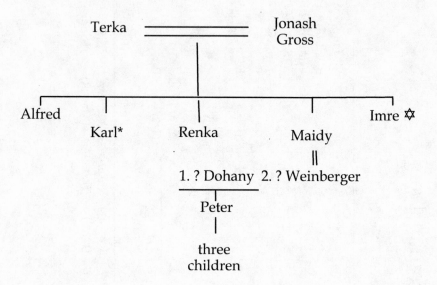

Footnotes refer to page 295.

[1] Ignatz was married twice and divorced twice.

[2] Herman was injured in the war and died in a sanitarium.

[3] David married Regina Rubenstein and had three children.

[4] Joseph married Kato and had two children; killed by the Hlinka Guard in Nitra.

[5] Margit married a Mr. Bogengluck and had three children. Died in the Holocaust.

[6] Toyvie married twice and divorced twice.

*Karl was married twice. His first family was killed during the war. Karl later remarried and had a son, Paul.

✡died in the Holocaust

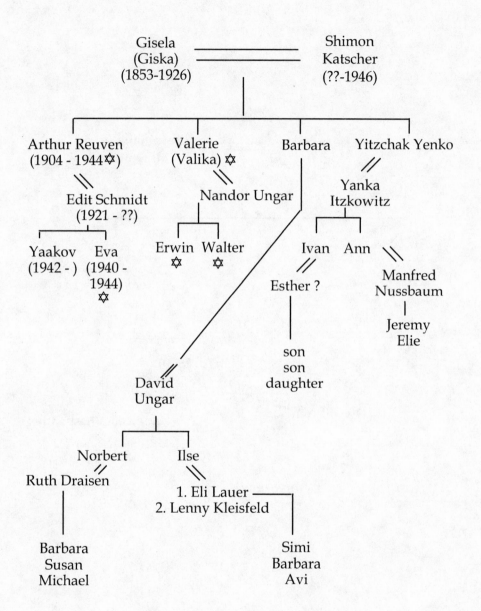

✡died in the Holocaust

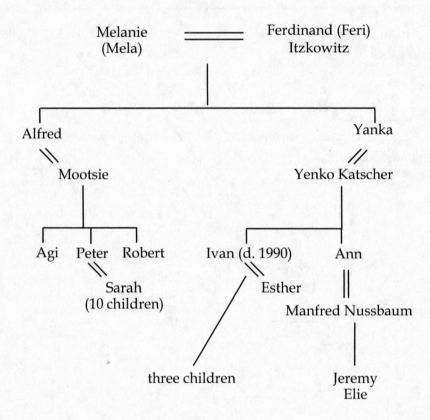

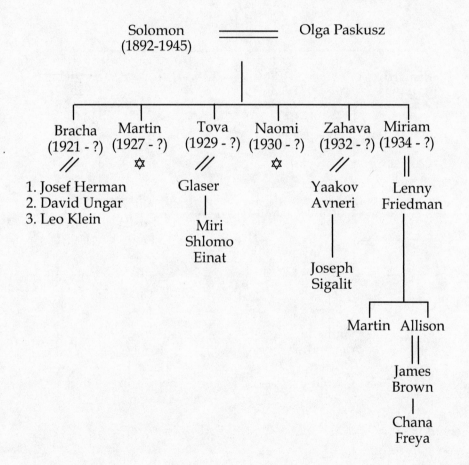

Solomon
(1892-1945) ═══════ Olga Paskusz

| Bracha (1921 - ?) | Martin (1927 - ?) | Tova (1929 - ?) | Naomi (1930 - ?) | Zahava (1932 - ?) | Miriam (1934 - ?) |

1. Josef Herman
2. David Ungar
3. Leo Klein

Glaser

Miri
Shlomo
Einat

Yaakov
Avneri

Lenny
Friedman

Joseph
Sigalit

Martin   Allison

James
Brown

Chana
Freya

✡died in the Holocaust

A Candle in the Heart — 299

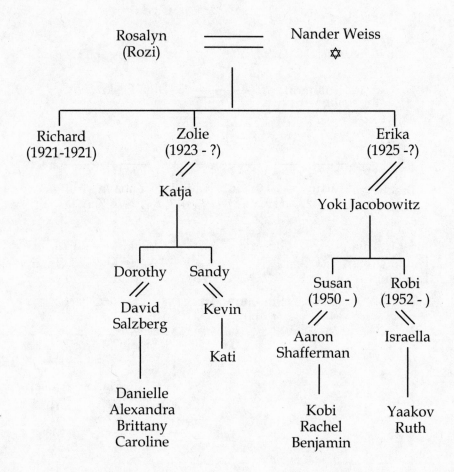

✡died in the Holocaust

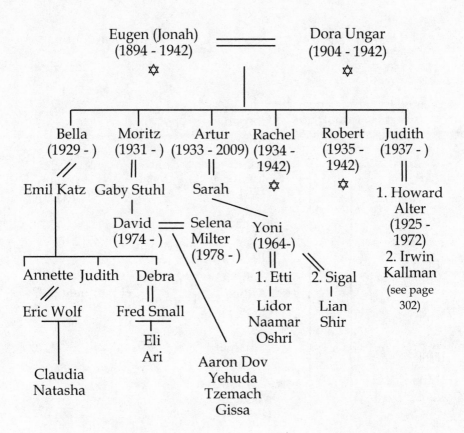

Eugen (Jonah)
(1894 - 1942)
✡

Dora Ungar
(1904 - 1942)
✡

Bella
(1929 -)
//
Emil Katz

Moritz
(1931 -)
||
Gaby Stuhl

Artur
(1933 - 2009)
||
Sarah

Rachel
(1934 -
1942)
✡

Robert
(1935 -
1942)
✡

Judith
(1937 -)
||
1. Howard
Alter
(1925 -
1972)
2. Irwin
Kallman
(see page
302)

David
(1974 -) === Selena
Milter
(1978 -)

Yoni
(1964-)
||
1. Etti
|
Lidor
Naamar
Oshri

2. Sigal
|
Lian
Shir

Annette Judith
//
Eric Wolf

Debra
||
Fred Small
|
Eli
Ari

Claudia
Natasha

Aaron Dov
Yehuda
Tzemach
Gissa

✡died in the Holocaust

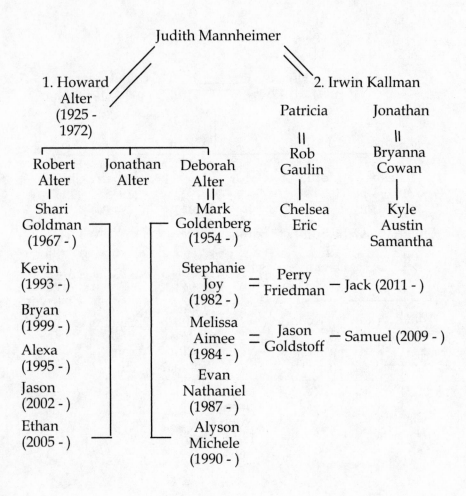

Judith Mannheimer

1. Howard Alter (1925 - 1972)

2. Irwin Kallman

Robert Alter
|
Shari Goldman (1967 -)

Jonathan Alter

Deborah Alter
||
Mark Goldenberg (1954 -)

Patricia
||
Rob Gaulin
|
Chelsea Eric

Jonathan
||
Bryanna Cowan
|
Kyle
Austin
Samantha

Kevin (1993 -)

Bryan (1999 -)

Alexa (1995 -)

Jason (2002 -)

Ethan (2005 -)

Stephanie Joy (1982 -) = Perry Friedman — Jack (2011 -)

Melissa Aimee (1984 -) = Jason Goldstoff — Samuel (2009 -)

Evan Nathaniel (1987 -)

Alyson Michele (1990 -)

Selected Document List
Mannheimer ~ Ungar Families

Mannheimer

Birth record index — Moritz Manheimer - 29 April 1853 - Bratislava State Archives (Piestany, Jewish Congregation Records - Births 1852-1884)

Hungary: All Citizens Census, 1869 - Postyen, Nyitra - Isak Monheimer - abt 1818

Marriage record index - Moritz Manheimer - 30 December 1878 - Bratislava State Archives (Piestany, Jewish Congregation Records - Marriages 1852-1883)

Birth record index — Jona Manheimer - 18 January 1894 - Bratislava State Archives (Piestany, Jewish Congregation Records - Births 1890-1940)

Marriage Extract - Jeno Manheimer & Dora Ungar - 12 December 1928 - Republic of Hungary, Register of Marriages

Death Extract - Dora Mannheimer - 10 July 1944 - Republic of Hungary, Register of Deaths

Fischer

Hungary: All Citizens Census, 1869 - Nagy-Rippeny, Nyitra - Sigmund Fischer - abt 1825

Ungar

Marriage Record - Dunajska Streda, Slovakia - Moritz-Mose Ungar & Eszter Abelesz - 12 December 1866 - Hungarian National Archives

Marriage Record - Dunajska Streda, Slovakia - Simon Ungar & Zilli K-lein - 30 October 1867 - Hungarian National Archives

Hungary: All Citizens Census, 1869 - Nagy-Czeteny, Nyitra - Jonas Ungar - abt 1869

Birth Record - Dunajska Streda, Slovakia - Jonas Ungar - 7 March 1869 - Hungarian National Archives

Birth Record - Dunajska Streda, Slovakia - Izrael Ungar - 1 July 1870 - Hungarian National Archives

Birth Record - Dunajska Streda, Slovakia - Mari Ungar - 2 March 1873 - Hungarian National Archives

Birth Record - Dunajska Streda, Slovakia - Iczig Wolf Ungar - 31 August 1874 - Hungarian National Archives

Birth Record - Dunajska Streda, Slovakia - Unknown Ungar - 5 June 1876 - Hungarian National Archives

Birth Record - Dunajska Streda, Slovakia - Izrael Ungar - 23 May 1878 - Hungarian National Archives

Death Record - Dunajska Streda, Slovakia - Jakab Ungar - 28 January 1881 - Hungarian National Archives

Death Record - Dunajska Streda, Slovakia - Itzig Wolf Ungar -1 December 1894 - Hungarian National Archives

Birth Extract - Dora Ungar - 23 February 1904 - Republic of Hungary, Register of Births

Death Extract - Etelka Ungar - 10 July 1944 - Republic of Hungary, Register of Deaths

Neuman

Hungary: All Citizens Census, 1869 - Nyitra, Nyitra - Jos.
Neuman - abt 1808

Death Extract - Regina Neumann - 10 November 1911 -
Republic of Hungary, Register of Deaths

NOTES

I used a number of resources to flesh out historical events.

I thank the YIVO Institute for Jewish Research for the use of its archives; the AMIT Children's Organization (Americans for Israel and Torah—formerly Mizrachi Women of America) for access to their materials, and The Simon Wiesenthal Center in Los Angeles for its on-line Multimedia Learning Center. I also wish to thank Yad Vashem and the United States Holocaust Memorial Museum for use of their on-line resources.

Piešťany sits on the Váh River in Western Slovakia. To the east, the Považský Inovec mountain range shields the town from the harshest winds; to the west, a wide strip of flat plain stretches for miles to a set of hills, while to the south lies the fertile Danubian plain and the major city of Bratislava.

Since the time of the Roman Empire, the hot, sulfurous spring waters of Piešťany oozing up through a thin layer of mud were considered therapeutic and, at the end of the 19th century, spa facilities were

SLOVAKIA

built to take advantage of that. At the same time, the city fathers developed sporting events and urged professional associations to hold their conferences in town. Cultural activities followed—concerts, plays and exhibitions—and soon Pieštany became a major resort in Central Europe. Many members of the continent's royal families "took the waters" in Pieštany, and celebrities—like Ludwig van Beethoven—were enthusiastically welcomed.

The first record of Jews in the town dates to 1736; 12 Jewish families lived under the patronage of Count Forgacs. In 1756 there were but three families; eighteen years later, in 1774, there were 24 Jewish families and a synagogue. By 1795, there were 50 Jewish families in Pieštany.

Antisemitic violence flared when Czechoslovakia was formed in 1918, but President Tomáš Masaryk and Foreign Minister Eduard Beneš forcefully opposed it. Their example and influence sent the antisemitism back underground, only to have it resurface again in 1920.

The Europa Plan
and the Attempt to
Save Hungarian Jewry

The Slovakian underground Jewish Rescue Committee headed by Rabbi Chaim Michael Dov Weissmandl and Gizi Fleischmann, a Zionist activist, negotiated with Dieter Wisliceny, the Nazi advisor on Jewish affairs in the German Embassy in Bratislava, and arranged a $50,000 bribe for him and several Slovak leaders in order to save 20,000 Slovakian Jews. (They later tried to implement something called The Europa Plan to rescue all of Hungarian Jewry, and made the original arrangements for what came to be known as the Kasztner Train, arrangements debatably responsible for saving the lives of approximately 20,000 Hungarian Jews toward the end of the war.) Fleischmann was killed in Auschwitz, as was Weissmandl's immediate family. However, he jumped from one of the cattle trains and escaped, eventually making his way to America, where he rebuilt the Nitra Yeshiva in Mt. Kisco and called it The Yeshiva Farm Settlement. My Aunt Giska moved to Mt. Kisco as well, and the Nitra students fondly referred to her as Katscher *Néni* (Auntie Katscher).

A note about Carl Lutz, who saved many Jews with fake *Schutzpasses*: After the war, Swiss officials refused to acknowledge Lutz's valor; he was even accused of having "exceeded his competences" for forging the protective letters. Yad Vashem declared him a Righteous Gentile, and he was honored in

Hungary with a plaque on Dob Street, near the Dohany Synagogue. He died in 1975.

JDC Child Care in Slovakia

The Joint Distribution Committee (JDC) operated in Czechoslovakia from early April 1945 until the Government Order of the Ministry of Foreign Affairs requiring JDC to cease operations by 31st January 1950. Quarterly reports of activities in Czechoslovakia including Slovakia were published throughout this period.

Villa Sylvia, Tatra Mountains. The first JDC report in 1945 described the use of the Home as a convalescent facility where 127 children had stayed during July 1945 for various periods.

It had originally been set up and operated by the World Jewish Congress, later taken over and subventioned by AJDC. Larger facilities were leased during 1946, and the Children's Home appears in reports as a JDC funded orphanage through 1946. 67 children—orphans or partial orphans were reported living there aged 6 to 16 from the Czech lands and from Slovakia. The majority of the children in the home were survivors or had been in long term hiding and were undernourished and suffering other ill effects and problems. The home was under regular medical supervision and the health of the children was monitored. They received medical care including vitamins, tonics and medicines as needed. Many started to thrive in the air of the Tatra Mountains.

JDC continued funding the orphanage. In June 1947 an agreement was reached with the World Jewish Congress regarding childcare activities in European countries and on 1 July 1947 WJC turned over Villa Sylvia Children's Home to be administered by SVAZ (Union of Jewish Communities in Slovakia). The agreement maintained that JDC would finance Villa Sylvia through SVAZ.

By 1947 some 30 children were registered in the home mostly orphans or half orphans. JDC made regular inspections and covered the budget. Children in the home were mainly concentration camp survivors and needed special medical care. In December 1947 a new orphans home was established at Nove Mesto in a building which formerly served as a Home for the Aged, with a maximum capacity of 45 children from the ages of 6 to 15. Many applications were received and a careful assessment was made before offering places. Many of the children were orphans or had one parent alive and efforts were made to encourage and retain contact with a surviving parent or relative. Detailed reports of the home and facilities appear in JDC quarterly reports. Children living in the home attended local day schools supplemented by Jewish and other cultural activities. Courses in sewing, knitting, typewriting, bookbinding etc. were provided and included practical training. Medical health was regularly monitored; a Jewish pediatrician was employed by the Home and a child welfare officer employed by SVAZ.

The Nove Mesto Orphans Home replacing the Sylvia Home in the Tatra Mountains had become Ohel David in 1948. All school aged children were transferred to the Nove Mesto Home and there was a waiting list. It was thought that many children would emigrate allowing the transfer of another group of younger children who were waiting to be placed. Some children had emigrated to England and Ireland. As 1948 progressed it was assessed that the need in the future for such a home would not be a priority. Plans were being made to convert the orphanage into a cultural home for children from provincial areas. The Home continued to be subventioned by the JDC. Meanwhile the Sylvia Home in the Tatra Mountains had also continued to operate through 1948 as a recreation center for social cases, supported by SVAZ but plans were also made to close it completely and some ten children living there were to be transferred to Nove Mesto by January 1949.

Before the War Rabbi Armin Frieder (1911–1946), Slovakian rabbi in Nove Mesto and member of the underground had been involved with the Ohel David home for the aged which had become a refuge and shelter for many people from the deportations. Adminstrator of the Home was Armin Vogel. A post-war commemorative plaque was put on the building which once housed the Ohel David Aged home.

This report was compiled from JDC Quarterly Research reports & files CZ.96, CZ.108 CZ.113,CZ.115;Wiener Library News Bulletin No. 49 November 2005.

The Kindertransports

The *Kindertransports* were the brainchild of Rabbi Dr. Solomon Schonfeld, an Englishman who was the principal of a small Jewish day school in London, and the same Rabbi Weissmandl of the Jewish Committee that had saved us from the Hlinka Guard in Žilina. Schonfeld was a close friend of the rescue activist from Nitra and had been his student before the war. He had also been a friend of the Katscher family and had stayed with them when he was studying at the yeshiva in Nitra.

Galvanized into action by an eloquent and anguished plea Weissmandl sent him in April 1938, Schonfeld decided to focus on rescuing as many Jewish children as he could in any way possible. Weissmandl's letter asked Schonfeld to let the world know that the Jews of Austria's *Shevah Kehillot*, the "Seven Communities," had been deported by the Nazis and their collaborators and dumped on the Polish border. Systematically starved and beaten, with no country willing to accept them, Jews were dying, many were dead and many more were in dire straits.

In his letter he asked, "Is your heart made of stone that you don't melt?"

When I was younger, and before I knew I was going to write this book, I was asked to write an anecdote for a book about Schonfeld by the late scholar Dr. David Kranzler. At that time, I hadn't done my research, hadn't asked my siblings for clarification of my hazy memories and basically relied on myself to tell my story—sometimes erroneously, as it turned out. Dr. Kranzler's book, *Holocaust Hero*, published by Ktav, is about how Rabbi Dr. Schonfeld's *Kindertransports* came to be and about all the amazing things he did to save 4,000 people before, during and after the Holocaust.

Following Weissmandl's instructions, Schonfeld led publicity campaigns and essentially became a one-man British rescue commission who enlisted, begged, borrowed and somehow managed to get help from every quarter of British society—from the Jewish community to Windsor Castle, from the House of Lords to simple country villagers.

When *Kindertransports* were first organized in 1938 in Vienna by Jewish organizations, Weissmandl noticed that Orthodox children were being left out, so he contacted Schonfeld and asked him to organize *Kindertransports* for Orthodox Jewish children. By the time he was stopped, Schonfeld had brought 3,000 Orthodox children from Vienna to England, personally sponsoring each child. At one point, there were at least 35 children living in the house he shared with his mother and brother—a house where every extra space held a cot for a child. He himself slept on a small cot in the attic.

Schonfeld, who eventually married the Chief Rabbi's daughter, founded the Chief Rabbi's Religious Emergency Council, known as the CRREC, and continued his rescue attempts, while sending relief and emergency aid to the victims.

When the carnage was finally over in Europe, he went back to find the lost children he knew had to be there—the hidden Jewish orphans most of all. And then he did even more for the displaced persons in the many camps scattered across Western Europe, while simultaneously making sure the thousands of children he brought to England were properly cared for.